How to Become
A GREAT CREATIVE GENIUS

Judith Anne Still

The Phoenix Rising Series

THE MASTER-PLAYER LIBRARY
Flagstaff, Arizona

All inquiries should be addressed to:
The Master-Player Library
P. O. Box 3044
Flagstaff, AZ 86003-3044

Library of Congress Catalog Card No. 2007922297

First Edition
Published in July 2007

Hardback
ISBN-13:   978-1-877873-19-5
ISBN-10:   1-877873-19-5

Paperback
ISBN-13:   978-1-877873-20-1
ISBN-10:   1-877873-20-9

PRINTED IN THE UNITED STATES OF AMERICA

Dedication

Gentle thanks to the many teachers in my experience who inspired humanity and divergent thinking in their students, notably Grace Dinges, Florence Sprenger, Gordon Vincent, Sheila Phillips, Dr. Sherwood Cummings and Dr. Ann Haaker.

How to Become
A GREAT CREATIVE GENIUS

Table of Contents

How to Become
A GREAT CREATIVE GENIUS

Table of Contents, cont.

FOREWORD

This book was originally meant to be a tribute to, and a discussion of, the musical achievements of American composer and conductor, William Grant Still. I meant, herein, to answer the questions, "What made the music of Still so very special," and "Why are Still's compositions works of genius?" It seemed to me that it was my job to consider these questions, because the child of an important person should be in a position to know how the parent worked, thought and believed, professionally, personally and philosophically.

However, as it sometimes happens, the form of the book soon became dictated by larger issues that overtook and consumed the initial idea. In order to understand the work of a creative genius, one must decide what qualities a creative person has that others do not have. It must be determined whether creativity is a gift from an outside source, or whether it comes from intelligence. Furthermore, the inquiring mind must decide whether genius is a trick of nature, or whether it can be cultivated.

After many hours of research into these complex problems, I found myself writing, not about a noted composer, but about genius itself, and about the ingredients of creative genius in particular. Happily, my father, William Grant Still, had himself occasionally written about the art of creation in his journals and articles, and so his words are frequently quoted to give legitimacy to the conclusions that are drawn. Without his opinions this volume would be nothing worth, for the author is not so much an expert on greatness as I am an admirer of it.

INTRODUCTION
Prepare to Fill the Need

[In our age of art and music,] inspiration is considered less important than mental gymnastics... . Wrote Boris Erich Nelson, ... "Too much steel and concrete [exists in American culture]. Steel and greed, concrete and selfishness of self-righteousness, which is even worse... a sparsity of approach and genuine 'heart'... ."

- William Grant Still[1]

We live in degenerate times. As the century progresses, we find that individuals do nothing that is truly individual or original. People are directed in all that they do by the media, by slogans, by the path of least resistance; most enterprising persons are bound by systems, by computer programs, and by the fastest means to obtain the largest profit.

The life of the young is in computer games, primitive rhythms, ...in the trivial, the commercial and the faddish. The

---

[1] Still, William Grant, "American Music and the Well-Timed Sneer," *Opera, Concert and Symphony* 13 [May 1948] 26-27.

schools talk about "originality" and "individualism," but we only imitate, and participate in, novelty. We have no Shakespeares, but we adapt and "improve" Shakespeare on the stage. Concert music is "dumbed down" for the masses, and emasculated to serve as elevator entertainment. (I was recently approached by a television executive who wanted to turn William Grant Still's grand opera, "Troubled Island," into a pop stage show.[2]) Explicit films and advertising art have replaced culture in our society. As Jacques Barzun (b. 1907), American historian of ideas and culture, describes our artistic milieu,

> Creative is industry jargon for words and ideas that go into an ad.[3]

Many intellectuals in the last fifty years have spoken with feeling about the lack of creativity in our age. Novelist H. G. Wells (1866-1946), in *Mind at the End of Its Tether*, complained that humanity had become uncreative, inadequate, drugged, anaesthetized, cynical, self-consoling, self-interested and jaded.[4] Author and poet John Ciardi (1916-1986), while he admitted that creativity could not be taught, said that "creativity cannot spring from the untaught." The presumption with him was that our schools are not teaching the young

---

[2] Still's *Troubled Island* (1938) was produced by the New York City Center in 1949. It was the first opera written by an African-American to be produced by a major American opera company. Refer to Still, Judith Anne and Lisa M. Headlee, eds., *Just Tell the Story: Troubled Island* [Flagstaff, Arizona: The Master-Player Library, 2006].

[3] Barzun, Jacques, "The Paradoxes of Creativity," *American Scholar* [Summer 1989] 341.

[4] Wells, H. G. *Mind at the End of its Tether* [London: William Heinemann Ltd., 1945]; Well's last book, *Mind at the End of its Tether*, expressed pessimism about mankind's future prospects.

how to be creative, that is, how to "imaginatively" recombine old elements into new ones.[5]

One of the problems with us may be that history advances in cycles of barbarity and enlightenment, as civilizations move through the various cosmic personalities of the zodiac. Note, for instance, how the great age of Greek culture slipped into the sodden and vulgar Hellenistic period. Among the ancient Greeks, drama was integral to society. It provided moral precepts and spiritual understandings. Odysseus in Homer was between divine and mortal—a true hero with super-human power. Oedipus was a larger-than-life man of puissance and potency who was brought low by Godly intervention. His clash with fate taught audiences about the folly of pride and self-love. By the time that Hellenistic theater was in vogue, the popular heroes on the stage were notably unheroic: Jason appeared in plays as a puny, pathetic figure,[6] and Philemon's slapstick comedy and stock characters were more popular than Menander's philosophical drama.[7] The public simply wanted to be entertained on the most basic level possible; the arts and education had deteriorated to a lamentable degree.

And so it is in our time. Today, theater is not a necessity, and the low ebb of social concerns is reflected in our diminished dramatic presentations, harsh music, and disjointed or simplistic literary efforts. We might say,

---

[5] Ciardi, John, *Saturday Review*, December 15, 1956.

[6] The original characterization of the mythological Jason led a heroic quest for the Golden Fleece, a winged ram that would rightfully place him on the throne.

[7] The showy Greek comedies of Philemon (c362BC-c262BC) enjoyed popularity over those of his rival, Menander (c342 BC-291 BC), who focused on the everyday affairs of the people of Athens. Later times, however, have found Philemon's works unintelligible, and, it is thought that his successes might be attributed to malice, intrigue and professional jealousy.

therefore, that society gets what it deserves, or what most expresses itself. Heroes do not spring up where audiences are unheroic.

The English poet Sir William Watson (1858-1935) once said, "The sense of greatness keeps a nation great."[8] Thus the nation in which we live might well weep, for the nation and the world are without a sense of greatness. The huge sadness of contemporary culture is that it so often mistakes ego, or power, or wealth, or pomp, or superficiality or glitter, or mass appeal, for greatness. We have no lack of avarice, vanity, conflict, prurience, crudity and waste. For every simple heart there are a hundred who seek validity through control, abuse or notoriety. As the natural environment suffers and declines from the onslaughts of uncaring exploitations, we have, in a small window of opportunity between hope and annihilation, a chasm-deep need for heroes.

Greatness is needed, in leaders of nations, in exponents of the arts, in commercial businesses, and in scientific and medical integrity. Who will speak for the earth and its dwindling resources? Who will give gentleness to industry and statesmanship? Where shall we look for the saviors of the future? In what delusions and impulses have we lost our role models? Where abide the brightest and the best?

We talk endlessly of finances and leadership and glamour and media personalities, but who, at the bitter end, stands silent over the rich man's grave? Who mourns when the loudest voices fall silent? Who plays the music when the music has only been noise? Who covets the images of art that is not art? Few of the famous and the forceful are great, nor will they be long remembered. Yet one is not great if memory

---

[8] Sir William Watson's "Our Eastern Treasure," from "Ver Tenebrosum: Sonnets of March and April 1885," *National Review*, V [June 1885] 484-489.

preserves the name, for the name of Judas spans the centuries. Genius and greatness may not be of one blood. All geniuses are not great, and all great people are not geniuses.

Truly significant individuals have, in past ages, made the world a better place, and have inspired the masses to do more and to climb higher. They were often not wealthy or powerful, nor known to history. They invented the wheel, and metal alloys, and musical notation, and the arch and the dome, and irrigation systems. By their works, we have known them. As Howard Gardner put it, there is creativity with a "big C" and creativity with a "little c." Albert Einstein's (1879-1955) theory of relativity was creativity with a big C, changing "an entire field of thought." Lesser creativity has come from any persons anywhere when they make something that compares with the best in the world, or produce, or invent, or "put up the best performance we can—in anything, and only in so doing lies satisfaction in living."[9]

Among great humans in the past have been Rembrandt, Khalil Gibran, Herman Melville, Anne Morrow Lindbergh, and Mother Teresa—people who did not fear the unconventional, the nontraditional, the impossible, but who took traditional avenues and found new ways to traverse them, and new insights into them. We are much in need of such people at this point in time; we languish in the absence of heroism and artistic mastery. Who shall our memorable figures be in this century? By their works we shall know them, but who will have done the work and performed the incredible deeds that we will speak of 100 years from now? What auras shall cover the globe like external spring and nurture the years ahead as does the refulgent earth? How shall

---

[9] Cohen, Gene D., M. D., Ph.D., "C = Me²: The Creativity Equation that Could Change Your Life," *Modern Maturity* 43W, #2 [March-April 2000] 37.

we teach their lessons to our children? Of what shall these lessons consist?

Dr. Perry Buffington has made a good list of the ingredients of greatness, in an article about heroes and heroism. He concludes that heroism requires persons with courage, [practical] intelligence, skill, knowledge, expertise, daring, idealism, foresight, humanitarian goals, honesty, generosity, love, affection, kindness and gentleness.[10] Beyond these qualities, great people are not always appreciated, nor do they lead idyllic lives of ease and charm. They are not necessarily people with IQs on the level of genius, and they seldom learn their creative skills through traditional schooling.

Is it possible for ordinary and unintelligent people to develop these attributes? Yes, it is possible, and so very necessary. In the following pages we will attempt to hit upon the ways in which all of us can become exceptional and overachieving individuals, and what qualities will be present in those who meet the challenge. This preparation for heroism is required, for the new age of enlightenment which lies ahead.

---

[10] Buffington, Perry W., Ph.D., "A Matter of Heroics," *Sky Magazine* [April 1989] 75-79.

I

Forget What You
Learned In School

The objective mind, in carrying out the plan of the subjective mind, must hold to the abstract tone color impressed upon it. ...At best the results attained by the objective mind always fall far short of the beauty of the original impression.

...As far as I am concerned, musical composition is chiefly a subjective process.

- William Grant Still[1]

Part of the reason for the lack of greatness in our society is in the failure of our schools to nurture creativity: our educational systems prevent students from realizing their true potentials. All students differ from each other in terms of cognitive abilities, yet lessons and tests in schools assess only

---

[1] Still, William Grant, "The Art of Musical Creation," *The Mystic Light* (Rosicrucian Fellowship Magazine) [July 1936] 298-299.

certain kinds of intelligences such as memory, rote learning, and problem solving where there is only one right answer.

Indeed, there are intelligences outside of the logical, mathematical and linguistic that are normally measured by IQ tests and school performance. IQ tests do not indicate true intellectual potential, nor can they predict future occupational success. Many gifted students are not identified and their abilities are not observed because they do not do so well on intelligence tests.[2] Especially disregarded are students with practical intelligence, which means students who have dexterity, sensitivity, sense of direction, ability to perform when options are variable, flexibility, discretion, innovation, productivity and skill in negotiation.[3]

The visionary R. Buckminster Fuller (1895-1983) tells us that all human beings are born with a "superb inventory of...comprehending faculties—as well as objectively articulating capabilities—than have as yet been acknowledged to be the case by the present educational establishments' capability accrediting boards, much less by the political-social pressure groups, such as veterans' organizations and parent-teacher associations. We may soon discover that all babies are born geniuses and only become dégenuised by the erosive effects of...conventional" educational practices.[4] Keep in mind that Leonardo da Vinci employed all of the intelligence of genius, which our educational systems ignore, to transform our "physical and cosmological environments."[5]

---

[2] Lapan, Stephen S., *The Meaning of Intelligence: Implications for Gifted Education* [Flagstaff, Arizona: Center for Excellence in Education, 1989].

[3] Peters, Ronald J., "Practical Intelligence," *National Forum* LXVIII, #2 [Spring 1988] 12-14.

[4] Fuller, R. Buckminster, "Planetary Planning," *American Scholar* 40, #2 [Spring 1971] 285.

[5] Fuller, 286.

The fact that intelligence tests only evaluate certain abilities may lead students to feel that they can be successful in fields wherein they are less suited than they would be in others as yet undiscovered. Suppose, for example, IQ tests determine that a certain male student is good in mathematics, but not good in verbal communication. The tests ignore the fact that the student has a flair for musical composition and orchestration. The student is placed in a mathematics/computer-track program in high school and does well. He undertakes a course of study in math in college, because his teachers have promised success in the field. Once in college, however, the student finds that he is not happy, because he is not really first and foremost a dedicated mathematician. The IQ tests have pointed to only one of his abilities, but they have not been able to indicate a talent that could bring him lifelong satisfaction.[6]

The real problem with IQ tests, according to one theorist, is that people who are "exceptionally creative" are not especially intelligent. They are not geniuses in the strict sense: most have IQs of about 120. They are not academically motivated, and sometimes they act up in class, or seem not to understand what is being taught to them. They appear bored or inept in many cases. They have "interesting ideas," and yearn for approval, but teachers generally want them to give up their creative ideas in order to exist comfortably in the social order.[7] Schools and societies want these inventive students to think convergently—to proceed directly toward one right answer to problems—but they think divergently,

---

[6] Cohen, Ted, Ph.D., "A Non-Phi Bete's Comment on Higher Education in America," *The Key Reporter* 66, #4 [Summer 2001] 7.

[7] Lloyd-Jones, Richard, "Theoretical Problems in Studying Creativity and Composition," *College Composition and Communication* XXI, #3 [October 1970] 263-265.

finding many novel approaches to problems, or in denying the significance of problems.[8]

One professor has gone so far as to intimate that IQ tests, and traditional tests of verbal skills, are responsible for sidelining creative people in society. The imaginative student is demeaned because he does not conform to "acceptable patterns." His self-esteem and self-confidence remain unaffirmed and are often negated.[9] (In this context, it is appropriate to mention that Einstein was downgraded as a student for having what was perceived to be a writing deficiency.)

The crux of the situation is that IQ tests measure intelligences that are not used in "everyday problem-solving behavior;" they do not assess the "ability to deal with...variables in a cognitively complex manner," nor do thy test "central-nervous system efficiency."[10] Furthermore, IQ tests do not test self-esteem and individual initiative. People with low IQs who learn by experience (learning-by-doing) perform better on complex interactive tasks than do non-experts with high IQs.[11]

As we have said, because tests do not identify the creative student, he or she may seem to be a misfit. He or she has an independent approach to problems, has an urge to express unique speculations, is interested in details, new ideas, departures from stereotypes, and can see the unfamiliar in the familiar. Teachers who want students to give the right

---

[8] Anderson, Harold H., *Creativity and its Cultivation* [New York: Harper & Row, 1959] 160.

[9] Kressy, Michael, "The Community College Student: A Lesson in Humility," *College English* 32, #7 [April 1971] 775.

[10] Doris, John L. and Stephen J. Ceci, "Varieties of Mind," *National Forum* LXVIII, #2 [Spring 1988] 22.

[11] Doris and Ceci, 22.

answers to questions and to memorize lists of data, do not reach the creative child. Author-poet John Ciardi has claimed that creativity can not be taught,[12] but perhaps the failure is in the lack of teaching techniques that call for creative thinking.

In the annals of history and psychology, we often discover persons who have mental, physical and situational handicaps who achieve far more than individuals with quick minds and high IQs. Thomas Edison, Andrew Carnegie, Abraham Lincoln, Booker T. Washington, Helen Keller, Beethoven and Milton all overcame insuperable difficulties to attain success. It would seem that the will to rise to great heights, and the inspiration to think creatively, are necessary for the cultivation of genius, while cleverness and intelligence are not.

Actually, more children than ever before in history lack the mind skills necessary to score adequately on IQ tests. The depletion of the world's soils, the use of toxic chemicals in farming, the diminution of nutrients in foods through excessive processing and preservation, have doomed children to mindlessness. According to *The Medical Post*, the intellectual ability of infants can be impaired by 80% if the mother is malnourished during pregnancy. If the mother does not take in enough essential fatty acids, the child's brain will be permanently underdeveloped, since 70% to 80% of brain cell division occurs before birth.[13] If the mind of the child is handicapped, it is especially important for classrooms to engage youngsters in learning through the senses, the emotions and through abilities other than convergent thinking skills.

---

[12] Ciardi, *Saturday Review*.
[13] Maurice, John, "Essential Fatty Acids Very Important to Fetus," *The Medical Post* [November 30, 1982] 29.

In order to become creative thinkers, children should be involved in problem-solving, in-depth understanding and in developing meaningful patterns of expression toward a larger goal. All five senses should be involved in learning by the use of varied stimuli. Students should observe, report, compare, interpret, classify, evaluate, summarize and deal with ambiguity. They should generalize, synthesize and prioritize in working with multiple factors.[14]

Schools will continue to teach mathematical, scientific, linguistic and logical skills, but they should also add divergent thinking skills. Students should be asked to deal with implications, explication and decision-making. Really successful people learn how to shape their environments, rather than how to adapt to them: they can cultivate the ability to impact their surroundings by learning to plan strategies, to prioritize lists of actions to take in emergencies, to plan the building of a business or organize group projects. They can learn to recognize their own strengths and weaknesses, and how to enhance their strengths and compensate for weaknesses.[15] In addition, lessons in musical intelligence, bodily intelligence, and bodily and mental dexterity should be offered, including instruction in music, dance, craftsmanship, debate, and puzzle-solving.[16]

Another addition to school curriculums should be in the area of exercising the imagination. Schools at present do not encourage students to think and explore imaginatively — they

---

[14] Herrold, Jr., William G., "Brain Research: Brain-Compatible Learning," *Educational Horizons* 68, #1 [Fall 1989] 39-41; Dirkes, Ann M., "Only the Gifted Can Do It," *Educational Horizons* 59, #3 [Spring 1981] 140.

[15] Sternberg, Robert J., "Beyond IQ Testing," *National Forum* LXVIII, #2 [Spring 1988] 11.

[16] Gardner, Howard, "Beyond the IQ: Education and Human Development," *National Forum* LXVIII, #2 [Spring 1988] 5-6.

ask students to replicate what is apprehended in the senses.[17] If imagination is encouraged in school, creative ability will not be far behind.

In truth, imagination and creativity are very close to each other in function and result. Tom Peters (b. 1942), an expert and best-selling author on business management practices, once defined creativity as "being in one setting and seeing something strange someplace else."[18] Peters' definition was, surprisingly, nearly identical to the psychologists' description of imagination, which is, in sum, the power to form mental images of that which is not actually present, and to make real that which is not.[19] To the psychologist, imagination is the "creative force" that frees people from "material limitations,"[20] meaning that creativity and imagination are essential to each other. To some academicians, inspiration is the substance to which creativity gives form and meaning.[21] Specifically, imagination may picture the ocean as "the heaving bosom of mother earth," whereupon the creativity of the poet will work the image into a poem.

The catalytic power of the creative imagination should be recognized by educators, and lessons should be developed that will build that power. The importance of such learning is indicated by the fact that no less a genius than Albert Einstein believed that the human imagination was more vital to humanity than science. Imagination, impelled by creativity,

---

[17] Eisner, Elliott W., "Celebration of Thinking," *National Forum* LXVIII, #2 [Spring 1988] 31-32.

[18] Editorial, Interviews with Creative People, "The Creators," *Modern Maturity* 43W, #2 [March-April 2000] 42.

[19] Chase, Loriene, Dr., "Casebook of Dr. Chase," *Westways* 77 [January 1985] 62.

[20] Chase, 63.

[21] Lerner, Gerda, "The Necessity of History and the Professional Historian," *National Forum* LXII, #3 [Summer 1982] 37.

perceives and communicates to others the glory of human worth, and gives meaning to that which has been, and inspires that which will be.

Imagination and creative perception may in fact become more and more useful in the millennium, even for scientific investigations. Werner Heisenberg, Erwin Schrödenger, Neils Bohr, and other such scientific giants, working in the area of quantum and wave mechanics, have demonstrated effectively that many phenomena which can be mathematically calculated and understood, can not be seen visually or microscopically. They can only be conceived of by the inner eye of the imaginative investigator.[22]

In our schools, and in our individual attempts to improve ourselves, we can elevate our brains and our creative abilities. The brain is constituted to improve itself, and may completely refashion "its internal synaptic structure every few days," or even every few seconds.[23] The old belief that nerve cells in the brain never regenerate may be false. We absolutely know that the contacts between nerve cells (synapses) change as we learn, and they change in function as we use them in learning.[24] As we learn to think, our thoughts trigger "storms of biochemical activities" in the brain that are multi-dimensional.[25] As we learn to think creatively, we can generate "a lot of different ideas from a single starting point... ."[26]

In other words, the more that we learn to think divergently, the more the human brain will expand to

---

[22] Miller, Arthur I., "On the Limits of the IMAGination," *National Forum* LXIII, #1 [Winter 1983] 26-28.

[23] Teitelbaum, Sheldon, "The Last Frontier," *USC Trojan Family* 22 [November 1989] 24.

[24] Teitelbaum, 25.

[25] Teitelbaum, 24.

[26] Peters, Ronald J., "Practical Intelligence," 16.

facilitate continued and increased creativity. Brain capacity will be more receptive to subconscious and subjective awareness. In the words of Dr. Gene D. Cohen, a leading researcher in the field of creativity and aging, "brain cells sprout new extensions" when responding "to a more stimulating or challenging environment... ."[27] Every new skill that is learned helps, especially new skills that involve language or music. In a study in 1963, for example, it was discovered that academically-talented students who learned to type "showed significantly greater gains in creative writing and creative thinking" than those who did not.[28] The same was true of students who learned to play a musical instrument.

Furthermore, the glory of divergent learning and thinking is in its cumulative value, and in its ability to lend itself, in adults, to what we call "wisdom." Pioneering researcher in the field of neurobiology, Lawrence C. Katz, Ph.D. (1956-2005, formerly at Duke University Medical Center), said that adults over 50 years of age "are better at solving problems, more flexible in their strategies, and better able to keep their cool during a crisis than younger people are."[29] They have developed wisdom owing to their harvesting of a "rich network of associations developed through a lifetime of experiences."[30] This rich network comes from divergent experiences, not from rote learning in traditional classroom settings.

---

[27] Cohen, Gene D., M. D., Ph.D., "Contemplating Creativity," *AARP Bulletin* 38, #4 [April 1997] 2.

[28] Denby, Robert V., "ERIC Abstracts and ERIC Indexes: Shortcuts to Creative Writing Documents," *English Journal* 58, #1 [January 1969] 140.

[29] Griffin, Kelly, "Brainpower," *AARP Magazine*, 48, #5B [September-October 2005] 77.

[30] Griffin, 77.

The bottom line in all of the research about learning and the human brain, is that both teachers and students should forget all that was once said about the importance of learning the "basics" — the 3Rs — in school. Those who wish to develop great creativity and genius should spend just as much time studying the liberal arts as they do mastering computers, math, reading and spelling. They must learn to read music and to play different styles of music; they must learn a second and a third language, and delve into theater, dance, debate, chess playing, and all aspects of an enriched curriculum. Outside of class, participation in environmental activities and community service groups will bring growing mental capacities into line with world order and benefit.

When steps are taken to legitimize creativity and inspiration over and above IQ, society will see new and magnificent heroes and artistic geniuses coming to life and beginning to produce all that is true and beautiful for the future of the globe. The time for these changes has been long in coming. William Grant Still commented on the long road through intellectual sterility in this manner:

> Mathematical formulae were often used by certain of the leading contemporary composers as a basis for musical creation... . The intellect usually took precedence over the emotions, and while intellect is necessary to musical creation, it should be no more than subordinate to inspiration... . But the horizons must broaden... [because]...just as the spark of freedom burns in the hearts of people all over the world...so does the inner love of beauty, and so does the public appreciation of all that is worthy in the arts.
> ...Experience has taught me that the ability to induce the flow of inspiration is of the greatest importance, for without it one's efforts often have little value.[31]

---

[31] Still, William Grant, "Modern Composers Have Lost Their Audience: Why?" *Australian Musical News* [July 1956].

II

Pursue Individual Interests
Be an Individual

I do think that it would be much better if we were to do more to develop individualism in music. ...The proponents of various schools of musical thought—[such as the proponents of] twelve-tone and serial music, and so on, you find that they will devote themselves entirely to that form of expression. For my part, ...I don't believe it. I think that every individual should remember that he's an individual, and [he should] give vent to expressing what he feels... .

- William Grant Still[1]

The great person believes in individual effort, and in what can be accomplished by one entity, unaided. Even the largest of tasks are not so daunting that they will not be tackled successfully by exceptional persons. A case in point is that of Samuel Johnson (1709-1784), who finished compiling his

---

[1] Brown, R. Donald. *William Grant Still: An Oral History* [California State University, Fullerton, California, 1967] 44-45.

magnificent dictionary of the English language in only seven years. He was a genius, of course, but he was an autonomous genius.[2] By contrast, the French government hired 40 geniuses of the French academy to put together the French dictionary, which project took the august gentlemen 55 years to complete.[3]

Singular, world-changing people almost always work alone. Dr. Johnson worked alone on his dictionary because he hoped that the compendium would sustain him financially, yet his self-interested need for profit did not mean that the result of his labor did not serve the common good. The individual efforts of great or heroic persons consistently uplift or advance the human cause. Dictators may work independently of others, as artistic people do, but their efforts largely sustain only their own ends; even their public service enterprises are designed to promote control, not to supply normal recompense for deeds well-done.

Among politicians and national leaders who succeed in war, and in various government programs, the greatest rewards come to those who rely on individual effort. In 1756, the Elder William Pitt, Prime Minister of England, won a war against France by taking over all the powers of the British government, and by refusing to consult with, or take advice from, his cabinet. In like fashion, Winston Churchill led the British participation in World War II with an attitude that assumed total independence from all controls and influences.

---

[2] Samuel Johnson was one of England's greatest literary figures. He was a poet, essayist, biographer, lexicographer, and literary critic. *A Dictionary of the English Language,* perhaps Johnson's best-known work, was written between 1747 and 1755.

[3] Finneran, John P., "A Tale of Two Dictionaries," *The Freeman* 43 [January 1993] 483-485.

Churchill's attitude, however, was vindicated by the outcome of the war, when the value of individualism was underscored. In all fields of endeavor, greatness can not exist without absolute freedom of expression, and uniqueness of style. Especially is this true in the arts. Indeed, artist Michael Hurd has stated that creative genius is the result of a "search for individuality," and the ultimate discovery of the inner voice and personality of the artist in that which is created. The work of art must reflect the artist, not society, and the artist must satisfy himself or herself first and foremost, and not "pander to a common denominator of common taste… ."[4]

Educator Ann Dirkes echoed Hurd's view, when she suggested that gifted people are likely to have unique interests, to learn independently, and to attack problems not recognized by the majority. Gifted students need "unique circumstances for learning," and artistic geniuses also need freedom to experiment and create along lines peculiar to themselves.[5]

The great scientific thinker, Jacob Bronowski (1908-1974), asserted that the essence of life was distilled from him in the fact that he did not put a fence between one part of his mind and another. He urged students to investigate the whole of life, from science, to languages, to poetry, to music, in order to develop, like Albert Schweitzer,[6] "a reverence for life."[7]

The delightful aspect of individual creativity is that it gives color and personality to artistic works that are produced.

---

[4] Francis, Michael, "The Essence of Creativity: The Michael Hurd Interview," *Talk of the Town* [April-May 1996] 7.

[5] Dirkes, 139.

[6] Albert Schweitzer (1875-1965) was an Alsatian theologian, musican, philosopher and physician. He received the Nobel Peace Prize in 1953 for founding the Lambaréné Hospital in West Central Africa.

[7] Bronowksi, Jacob, "This I Believe," *The Spiritual Healer* [February 2006] 8-9.

It is owing to the personalities of particular pieces of artwork that experts can identify a Rembrandt portrait or a Titian, or that musicians can talk about the "grandiose soaring" of Wagner, and the "delicate, ethereal quality" in the music of Chopin.[8] One critic suggested that the soul of the composer was expressed in the unique qualities of a particular work. Chopin, for example, injected into his compositions his aristocratic refinements, and his "averson for all that was crude or grotesque...," as well as his "sweet profundity" and deep, "sad-loveliness."[9] Chopin himself was one who talked about the innovative characteristics in the work of Franz Liszt, explaining that Liszt, "was the first to introduce in his compositions that peculiarity which gives such unique color to his impetuosity and which he called 'tempo rubato,' an irregularly interrupted movement, subtle, keen, broken, languishing," then "flickering like a flame in the wind... ."[10]

Obviously, one of the most significant features of artistic genius is the intense identification of the artist with his or her creation. This is not to say that uninspired observers will not try to deny the uniqueness of great artists; often critics or professors will try to pigeonhole or categorize works of great beauty. Shakespeare is often taught simply as a neo-Classicist, or an exponent of the Baroque, or a humanist. Milton is studied as a representative of the religious views of 17th century society. A professor of mine once claimed that Robert Frost's poems were only valuable because they expressed the theories of Sigmund Freud, although no evidence showed that Frost was even aware of the Freudian psycho-sexual ideology.

---

[8] Anonymous, "Disagree on Greatest Composer," Los Angeles *Herald-Examiner*, April 20(?), 1940.

[9] DiPirani, Eugenio, "Grasping the Soul of the Composer," *The Etude* LI, #4 [April 1933] 240.

[10] DiPirani, 240.

William Grant Still's music has been compared to that of Debussy and Delius, and to other composers who had either knowingly borrowed from Still, or who were completely unknown to Still.

Regardless of this lack of sensitivity in many critics and scholars in the modern era, the unreplicatable nature of artistic genius ordains that it will reveal itself to enlightened audiences over time, if left free to express itself independently of mediocre and jealous influences. The individuality of William Grant Still was not fully prized in the late 20th century, but a few custodians of his legacy realized that his soul of creativity would be preserved in his music, even after his death. His wife and life-time collaborator, Verna Arvey, in a lecture to the Swedish Academy, promised that Still had an individual "personal idiom" that shone through his compositions, "despite the variety of styles he had employed when treating contrasting subjects.[11] Between 1950 and 1980, no one was hearing Still's music very much in the world, because recordings were rare and access to them was limited. However, when recordings and performances began to increase by the thousands, many music lovers came forth to praise the interest and originality and individuality of the composer. As one conductor expressed it,

The one thing that can be said of William Grant Still is that there is no other music like his.

- Frank Fetta, Conductor of the Marina Del Rey/
Westchester Symphony Orchestra, California.[12]

---

[11] Arvey, Verna. Lecture to the Swedish Academy, Los Angeles, California [November 15, 1948].

[12] Fetta, Frank, Conductor of the Marina Del Rey/Westchester Symphony Orchestra, California. Comments to the audience at a performance of Still's "Poem for Orchestra," July 2003.

Pursue Individual Interests
Become Interested in Many Things

William Grant Still advocated the "use of all the means of musical expression that are available" in the expression of the endless variety of the universe.

- R. Donald Brown[1]

[Your music is] down to reality and usefulness... [It has the] wonderful and endless variety of the world...

- George Frederick McKay[2]

William Grant Still captured the multiplicity of creation in his music, and in his private life. In his own little domestic environment, he built furniture and toys, gardened, did crosswords, made pictures using a typewriter, studied spiritualist and religious literature, wrote speeches, and read historical biographies. His wide interests made him one with

---

[1] Brown, 31.

[2] McKay, George Frederick. Letter to William Grant Still, August 24, 1949.

most of the other creative geniuses in the history of civilization.

The truly great individual can be frequently discerned by the broad range of his or her talents: the noble mind is captivated by many things, and is usually adept at performing diverse tasks. Hardin Craig, a well-respected professor of English in the mid-20th century, recognized the need of genius to diversify when he opposed the trend in post-graduate education toward specialization. He pointed out that the natural activity of the human brain was in diversification: the brain was capable of coordinating billions of "separate acts of ideation."[3] Specialization, insisted Craig, was "selfishness," undertaken for "personal gain," and it resulted in "indifference to the welfare of our fellow men."[4] He lamented that his students were no longer required to learn Latin, Greek, Old and Middle English, Old Norse, Old Middle English and High German, Gothic, Sanskrit and Hebrew. He recommended that, if youngsters wished to develop great minds, they should learn widely, think expansively, and "deny self."

As Hardin Craig was aware, seldom does one find a great mind that is not skilled at, or interested in, many things. The mad genius, E. T. A. Hoffmann (Ernst Theodor Wilhelm Hoffmann, 1776-1822), was a poet, a novelist, a composer, a conductor, a counselor-at-law, an assessor, an architect, a muralist, a cartoonist, and director of a Polish academy of music.[5] Frederick the Great of Prussia (1712-1786) was a general, writer-poet, flutist, and composer.

---

[3] Henry, Nicholas L., "Hardin Craig, Professor," *American Scholar* 40, #2 [Spring 1971] 307.

[4] Henry, 308.

[5] Rivette, Marc, "The Tales of E. T. A. Hoffmann" *Opera and Concert* 13, #8 [August 1948] 16-17, 26.

Frederick the Great was not the only political leader who was a musician. George Washington played the flute and the violin, and danced an elegant minuet. John Adams attended operas and concerts, and began the tradition wherein the Marine Band plays at the White House. Thomas Jefferson was a pianist, violinist, and dancer of minuets, and he declared openly that music was his "favorite passion."[6] Benjamin Franklin played the violin, 'cello, harp, guitar, composed music and invented the instrument called the armonica.[7]

Actually, Franklin's other talents, beyond music, are worth listing. He was a journalist, publisher, diplomat, electrician, "founder of the physics of liquid surfaces, discoverer of the properties of marsh gas, designer of the *chevaux de fries* which halted the advance of the British fleet on the Delaware, inventor of bifocal spectacles and of improved fireplaces, advocate of watertight bulkheads on ships and of chimney shafts for the ventilation in mines... ."[8] He was an economist, meteorologist, agriculturist, friend of medicine, swimmer, chess player, philosopher, businessman—and yet he attended school as a youth for less than two years.[9]

One outstanding talent of the 20th century, Yehudi Menuhin (1916-1999), an acknowledged virtuoso on the violin, suggested that the versatility of people like Franklin was divinely inspired. The genius, said Menuhin, "is compelled to his destiny" by a "divine spark," which gives him, in addition to a specialized skill, an "ability to comprehend all things" in

---

[6] Roberts, Allen and Juliet Bridgman, "America's Musical Presidents," *Music Journal* XXXII, #4 [April 1974] 16.

[7] Cooke, James Francis, Dr., "The Fabulous Doctor Franklin," Speech to the Kiwanis Club of Philadelphia [January 17, 1956] 11.

[8] Koestler, Arthur. *The Art of Creation* [New York: Macmillan Co., 1964] 686.

[9] Cooke, 11-12.

"the entire field of human experience and knowledge." He develops his peculiar abilities, but does not neglect other interests and skills. While a student of music, Menuhin practiced four hours a day, walked two hours a day, swam, bicycled, and developed "good habits of thought."[10]

The phenomenal conductor, Leopold Stokowski (1882-1977), "was interested in everything from politics to electronics. He was an adventurer in life, with insatiable curiosity and willingness to try new things."[11] It was Stokowski who liberated the American Symphony from many unnecessary traditions: he put violins on the left, 'cellos on the right, allowed players more freedom in breathing and bowing, he permitted audiences to clap when they wished to express approval, (and not only between pieces), and, because of his great love of children, he originated the idea of children's concerts.[12]

It should be evident, at this point, that most geniuses who do much good in the world are either musicians, or admirers of music. Also, there have been few musical greats who have not been multi-talented, and variously skilled. It might some day be discovered that an affinity for music is the most important attribute of greatness, and the one most likely to bring value to the efforts of creative artists. The significant result of an indulgence in multitudes of interests, experiences and skills, is that any such indulgence brings new components into works that are created, invented or envisioned.

Perhaps the most visible results of variety in interests, where creativity is concerned, can be found in the music of

---

[10] Brant, Leroy V., "Genius Begins with Maturity," *The Etude* 71, #11 [November 1953] 20.

[11] Kostelanetz, Andre, "Unforgettable Leopold Stokowski," *Reader's Digest* [January 1978] 101, 103.

[12] Kostelanetz, 104.

William Grant Still. Still, according to the experts, "succeeded in making a tasteful blend of all of the elements that had gone into his education,"[13] and into his diversions, so that he could finally bring "to music a new voice, a voice filled with lovely melodies, gorgeous harmonies, insidious rhythms and dazzling colors."[14] It was for this reason that Dr. Howard Hanson (1896-1981) dubbed Still "a great man," with "his own brand of personal genius."[15]

And composer Still, who was a generous person, willing to share his time and talent with others, would have been the first to suggest that, if wide-ranging activities did much for him, they could do the same for everyone else.

---

[13] Matthews, Miriam, "Phylon Profile, XXIII: William Grant Still--Composer," *Phylon* 22 [Atlanta, Georgia: Atlanta University Press, Second Quarter 1951]; or, Still, Judith Anne, ed. *William Grant Still and the Fusion of Cultures in American Music*, 2nd edition revised [Flagstaff, Arizona: The Master-Player Library, 1995] 199. Miriam Matthews (1905-2003) became the first librarian of Color in California when, in 1945, she was appointed head librarian to the Washington Irving Branch Library in Los Angeles. Matthews also led the push to revise the American Library Association's Bill of Rights in 1948, and she helped to interest the public in Negro History Week. In her personal life, she was the owner of one of the largest collections of Negro art in the country.

[14] Hanson, Howard, Dr. Keynote address: "A Tribute to William Grant Still," Testimonial Dinner For William Grant Still, Friends of Music, University of Southern California, Los Angeles, California, May 24, 1975; or, Still, Judith Anne, ed. *William Grant Still and the Fusion of Cultures in American Music*, 204. Dr. Howard Hanson (1896-1981), sometimes called the dean of American composers and conductors, became director of the Eastman School of Music in 1925 and won a Pulitzer Prize for his *Fourth Symphony* in 1944. He championed American composers in many significant concerts.

[15] Hanson, Howard, Dr. Introduction, *William Grant Still and the Fusion of Cultures in American Music*, edited by Judith Anne Still, 2nd edition revised, [Flagstaff, Arizona: The Master-Player Library, 1995] *i*.

III

Develop Courage, Determination and Practicality
Be Courageous and Determined

The composer's chief need is...determination—the drive to convert that burning urge [to express himself] into the kind of ceaseless, dogged effort that no obstacles can check.

- William Grant Still[1]

The great person in any field of endeavor has courage. As Seneca put it, "A king is he who fears nothing."[2] He might as well have said, "A king is he who acts as if he fears nothing,"

---

[1] Still, William Grant, "The Composer Needs Determination and Faith," *The Etude* 67 [January 1949] 7.

[2] Lucius Annaeus Seneca, or Seneca the Younger (c4 BC-65 AD), was a great Roman philosopher, statesman, writer and dramatist. He also served as a teacher and advisor to Nero, son of the emperor Claudius. Later, upon being accused of having been involved in a plot to murder the then-ruling Nero, he was forced by Nero to commit suicide by slashing his wrists and bleeding to death in the presence of friends. His wife, Pompeia Paulina, chose to follow her husband by ending her own life.

for even the greatest of us can have fear, yet it takes a giant to behave fearlessly.

Educators have stated that courage is one of the prime requisites for a creative artist. According to Richard Lloyd-Jones, creativity requires bravery and freedom from restriction, nor should it fail to brook the power of any accepted artistic traditions.[3]

Barbara Currier Bell endorses Lloyd-Jones' assertion, insisting that learning how to create is "risky" — the creative person must not be afraid to be wrong, to appear silly, or to be criticized for dealing with things that are unknown to the public.[4] Bell further indicates that education in our age does not encourage either creativity or the courage to delve into the unknown; learning in our schools, she complains, is "routine, repetitive, and receptive." Better it would be for teachers to guide students according to English poet John Milton's (1608-1674) dictum that, "The light which we have gained was given us, not to be ever staring on, but by it to discover onward things... ."[5]

Psychologists have analyzed the mental habitudes of leaders in society, and have determined that, among top executives, leading statesmen, athletic coaches and symphony conductors, there are common traits which, if developed, do insure success.[6] All leaders differ in personality, behavior and artistic ability, but they all have a few qualities in common, the most important of which is "intensity of purpose." They

---

[3] Lloyd-Jones, Richard, 266.

[4] Bell, Barbara Currier, "Lesson About Learning," *National Forum* LXVIII, #2 [Spring 1988] 34.

[5] From John Milton's *Aeropagitica*, 1644; Bell, 34.

[6] Nanus, Burt and Warren Bennis. *Leaders: The Strategies of Taking Charge* [New York: Harper & Row, 1985]; Swanbrow, Diane, "The Anatomy of Leadership," *USC Trojan Family* 18, #2 [October 1985] 19.

direct everything in their personal lives, and in the lives of the people they lead, to attain their goals, and they put people around them who share their "vision of where they are going and a firm sense of how to get there."[7]

This "intensity of purpose" is seen, not just in leaders of groups, but also in singular geniuses. Johann Sebastian Bach (1685-1750) was a man of dogged courage and determination where his craft was concerned. He gave up several employments when his patrons and employers tried to direct his expressive style, creativity and private life. He was, in fact, "not a man to brook any invasion of his personal freedom."[8]

Other composers have also been boldly defiant in the face of authority. Beethoven flew in the face of musical tradition and freed music from old ways of doing things. Luigi Cherubini (1760-1842), was told by the emperor Napoleon that his music was "too noisy," and "too German," and that it should have been more "tranquil," as to "gently caress the ear."[9] Cherubini replied to Napoleon, "I see, General, the music you like is the kind which does not hinder you from reflecting on affairs of State." Napoleon was not pleased with this reply, or with other encounters with Cherubini, hence he denied the composer the Cross of the Legion of Honour. Cherubini never forgave Napoleon, while he continued to express entitlement to his own opinions.

This sense of entitlement and courage in composers can also be found in great statesmen, orators, and writers. Abolitionist Frederick Douglass (1818-1895) said, "Greatness

---

[7] Swanbrow, "The Anatomy of Leadership," 19.

[8] Turner, Robert, "Bach," *Pavilion*, Los Angeles Music Center [Southern California Symphony Association, Los Angeles, California, 1964] 8.

[9] Schweisheimer, Waldemar, M.D., "Cherubini and Napoleon," *The Etude* LX, #8 [August 1942] 522.

does not come to any people on flowery beds of ease. We must fight to win the prize. ...The hardships and dangers involved in the struggle give strength and toughness to the character, and enable it to stand firm in storm.... ."[10]

Brigadier General Joshua Lawrence Chamberlain (1828-1914), hero of the battle of Gettysburg, was praised for his commitment to his mission, for his tenacity, and for his courage. He worked hard to overcome a speech defect (stammering), after which he pushed himself to develop into an exceptional orator and military leader. He went into six battles in front of his troops, and, in spite of grave wounds, returned to battle saying,

> It is true my incomplete recovery from my wounds would make a more quiet life desirable.... . But there is no promise of life in peace, and no decree of death in war. And I am so confident of the insincerity of my motives that I can trust my own life and welfare of my family in the hands of Providence.[11]

Chamberlain, and all other great men and women in history, have maintained an absolute idea of the justice of their works in the world, and they insist upon that idea and ideal regardless of the danger to themselves and to their future livelihoods. William Grant Still did likewise, defending the rectitude of his creative efforts, even when it meant that he might lose a publisher, or a job. (It should be noted, too, that for an African-American classical composer in the 20th century, jobs and publishers were scarce. Racism rendered any refusal of a Colored man to follow directions a precarious

---

[10] Douglass, Frederick. *Life and Times of Frederick Douglass* [Hartford, Connecticut: Park Publishing Company, 1881].

[11] Smith, Edward C., "Joshua Lawrence Chamberlain: From Antietam to Appomattox," *Lincoln Review* 11, #13 [Spring-Summer 1994] 44.

enterprise.) It is fair to say, therefore, that Still's courage was uncommon for a man of his situation. Even less common was the dignity and patience that he evidenced when he confronted someone in authority who wanted to change his musical ideas. In 1935, Still's publisher complained that his music was "uncommercial," and the suggestion was made that the exquisite two-piano piece, "Kaintuck'," be rearranged for solo piano. Still sent an immediate reply as follows:

> Your letter exhibits your innate straight-forwardness that makes me value your friendship so highly, and causes me to wish to retain it. But it also points to the necessity of a painful step on my part unless we are able to arrive at a clearer understanding.
> When you say, "Some of my pieces are most uncommercial in the sense in which the term 'commercial' is generally accepted." All of my efforts arise from the desire to express beauty. It is this same expression of beauty unmixed with thoughts of renumeration that constitutes the greatest reward that my efforts can offer me.
> *Kaintuck'*...can in no way be reduced so as to permit of effective performance on one piano. I hold tenaciously to this statement, not that I wish to be adamant, but because I do not want to see *Kaintuck'* spoiled. In fact, I prefer to leave it unpublished rather than to have it brought out in a way that would rob it of whatever effectiveness it possesses.

Suffice it to say that Still's piece "Kaintuck'," stayed as it was, and it remains as exquisite in form and content today as it was in 1935 when the publisher objected to it. Without the composer's courage, its beauty would not have remained. Without courage, greatness will cease to exist on the earth. So it was, and so it shall be.

Develop Courage,
Determination and Practicality
Be Practical

There is no substitute for keeping an open mind and for
analyzing both sides of a question...
No matter how sensitive we are to outside influences, we
should never allow them to throw us off balance.

- William Grant Still[1]

There is one peculiarity that must be understood about
courage: courage can not exist without practicality. Without
the practical element, courage becomes foolhardiness. It is
well to stand firm for one's convictions, but not to the
detriment of one's believability, integrity, or opportunities for
survival.

---

[1] Still, William Grant, "Horizons Unlimited," *William Grant Still and the Fusion of Cultures in American Music*, Robert B. Haas, ed. [Los Angeles: Black Sparrow Press, 1975] 122.

Practical intelligence is one of the several kinds of intelligence not measured by IQ tests, and it is one of the several attributes that is possessed by great people to a very high degree. Practicality is the ability to apprehend "the facts of a situation" in such a way as to "guide action towards a desired goal."[2] Practicality includes the sensitivity to assess the needs and interests of others, and the persistence, flexibility, decisiveness, tact and discretion to produce positive results, whatever the desired goal.

Practical persons are "action-oriented" but realistic: they are aware of their own skills and frailties and those of their colleagues, they are optimistic about their chances for success, but pessimistic about other people's biases and motives.[3] They have lofty ideals, and they develop strategies to realize these ideals in a step-by-step, down-to-earth manner. The way in which they operate to make their visions manifest is often called "common sense."

Many people of enormous genius have had common sense, including Goethe, Byron, Rubens, and Berlioz.[4] Probably the finest example of a historic figure who had practical intelligence was Benjamin Franklin (1706-1790). In his *Poor Richard's Almanac* (1757), Franklin promoted the precepts that guided his life: industry, self-control, frugality, determination, sensibility.[5] The creator of *Poor Richard* was an initiator and a builder who put energy into many practical projects: he established an adult school, and the first insurance company in America; he founded the American Philosophical

---

[2] Webster's Dictionary, as quoted by Roger J. Peters, "Working Smarter: The Business of Practical Intelligence," *National Forum* LXVIII, #2 [Spring 1988] 12.

[3] Peters, Ronald J., 12, 16.

[4] Barzun, 345.

[5] Cooke, "The Fabulous Dr. Franklin" Speech.

Society, the Philadelphia Library, the Philadelphia fire company, the first American magazine, and the first American hospital; he invented the open stove and a rare musical instrument, the armonica; he studied electricity, meteorology, agriculture, and economics, and he was the first to store electricity for use at a later time.

Franklin's versatility, and his common sense approach to every field of cultural and scientific endeavor, set the tone for the next two centuries of American ingenuity and creativity in the United States. It is unlikely that another genius of his singular nature will visit the earth again, but, of course, Franklin himself would warn us that skepticism about the future is a grave handicap, and that all things in the universe are possible.

In addition, Franklin's mottos, which he published in *Poor Richard's Almanac*, were a clear affirmation of the belief that anyone, and everyone, can learn to be both practical and intelligent. His directives about hard work and good sense were designed to teach practical intelligence. He said,

God helps them that help themselves.

Early to bed and early to rise,
Makes a man healthy, wealthy, and wise.

Never leave that till to-morrow which you can do to-day.

Plough deep while sluggards sleep.

It is hard for an empty sack to stand upright.

Experience keeps a dear school, but fools can learn in no other.

There never was a good war or a bad peace.

In sum, the thrust of Benjamin Franklin's teachings was that individuals who hoped for success should be frugal, avoid procrastination, be prompt and assiduous in business, and become aggressive in learning how to do many things and to acquire wide experience.

The difference between the practical person and the impractical person was evidenced by Franklin's response to a problem which existed in the streets of Philadelphia in the 18th century. In those days, prior to the development of public works projects, the unpaved streets of the city became clogged with mud when the rains fell, rendering passage difficult and inhospitable to cleanliness. Citizens complained about the muck and mire, but did nothing to address the issue. Franklin spearheaded a campaign to pave the market area near his home, collected a sort of tax to pay for street cleaning, and brought a bill to the Assembly to have all the streets of the city paved.[6] Franklin's attitude toward practical difficulties was to solve them by practical means. The impractical person, on the other hand, would have blamed business slumps on rain storms and impassable lanes, calling his problems "acts of God."

Each of us can learn to tackle obstacles head on, with a view to efficient solutions. All of us can study problems, interview experts, do research, and search for resolutions. Any one human being can attack dilemmas with both mental and physical energy, and there is no person who can not strive for thrift and modest living. We can all give up profligacy, frivolity, self-indulgence and waste of effort in order to seek personal growth. Once habits of practical endeavor are established, the upward aspiring future creative genius can

---

[6] Franklin, Benjamin. *The Autobiography of Benjamin Franklin* [New York: Random House, 1944] 144-145.

use these skills to turn a life-interest into "a creative, serious accomplishment worthy of study and high devotion as well as sacrifice."[7]

---

[7] Still, William Grant, "My Arkansas Boyhood," *Arkansas Historical Quarterly* 26 [Autumn 1967] 285-292.

IV

Cultivate Humility,
Simplicity and Humor
Be Humble and Simple

Truth: Blessed is he who[m] God keeps reminded of his utter helplessness.

- William Grant Still[1]

...the distinguished composer, William Grant Still, is singularly modest and retiring.

- Miriam Matthews[2]

William Grant Still, a genuine American composer, will become world famous. When he does, he will be the last person in the world to know it, or to believe it if the knowledge is thrust upon him.

- Verna Arvey[3]

---

[1] Still, William Grant, *Personal Journal*, #113.

[2] Matthews, "Phylon Profile, XXIII: William Grant Still;" or, Still, Judith Anne, ed. *William Grant Still and the Fusion of Cultures in American Music*, 195.

[3] Arvey, Verna. *Studies of Contemporary American Composers: William Grant Still* [New York : J. Fischer & Bro., 1939] 46.

In addition to having courage, great leaders and artistic heroes possess humility and a simplicity of nature and technique. While humility and fearlessness may seem to be at odds with each other, they are, in reality, two parts of the same whole, or two faces of the same personality profile.

Matthew in the Bible (XXIII, 12) promised, "Whosoever shall exalt himself shall be abased; and he that shall humble himself shall be exalted." Scottish writer and historian, Thomas Carlyle (1795-1881), wrote, "All greatness is unconscious, or it is little and naught."[4] Another author, whose name I have forgotten, said, "Humility is the hallmark of greatness, even as quietness is the prelude to power."

Religious scholar and cultural interpretator, Martin Marty (b. 1928), believes that geniuses "seek simplicity" in their lives and works; people who are truly outstanding do not clutter their behavior with self-importance, and they are not threatened by others, even if others try to control them.[5]

It is interesting to observe that many great men and women in history came from ordinary families: Moses, Jesus, Chaucer, Joan of Arc, Franz Schubert, Robert Burns, John Keats, Charles Dickens, George Washington Carver, Mark Twain, Albert Schweitzer, Thomas Edison, and scores of others stepped out of obscurity into the limelight. Their simple beginnings did not lead to an envious urge to strive for luxury and power, even when others who were born poor, such as Napoleon and Eva Perón, resented their humble origins so

---

[4] Carlyle, Thomas, *Westminster Review* #12 [London, 1838].

[5] Marty, Martin E., "Simplify Your Life!," *Reader's Digest* 116, #695 [March 1980] 79; Martin E. Marty was Professor Emeritus at the University of Chicago, teaching at the Divinity School for 35 years. He was also a Lutheran pastor in the Chicago area, president or director for several associations and institutions, and a prolific writer. He authored more than 50 books, and served as a columnist, editor and regular contributor to several news publications.

much that they were well-nigh rabid for social status. Truly inspired people are not influenced by their environments to be larger than life—they are greater than the sum of their parts by virtue of their purity, innocence, gentleness, honesty, graciousness and serenity of mind and heart.[6]

Even in the theater of war, there are heroes who possess substantive philosophical greatness. Many of the shining lights on both sides in the Civil War were deeply religious men who were quietly committed to the cause in which they served, and they were, also, supremely humble men: Abraham Lincoln, Joshua Lawrence Chamberlain, and Frederick Douglass were three such men. Abraham Lincoln, in particular, made it a point to avoid arrogance and to demonstrate respect for all people in all levels of society. When he was a clerk early in his career, he accidentally overcharged a woman 6¼¢ for the sale of goods. After work that night, he walked two or three miles to the woman's house to reimburse her for that amount. In World War II, many of those who fought the Nazis ideologically and otherwise were also simple men and women. Karl Barth (1886-1968), a Swiss theologian, pitted his faith in God's love against the Nazi allegiance to "the State." Dietrich Bonhoeffer (1906-1945), the pacificist who was executed for taking part in the conspiracy to kill Hitler, spoke up for the honesty and simplicity of his part in the assassination attempt. He wrote,

> To be simple is to fix one's eye solely on the simple truth of God at a time when all concepts are being confused, distorted and turned upside-down. It is to be single-hearted.[7]

---

[6] Marty, 80.
[7] Marty, 80.

It may be surprising to find humility among great warriors, but it is well to remember that to be self-effacing is not to be powerless. Neither does it indicate a lack of intellect, for scientific geniuses and social philosophers have also been single-hearted and simple of purpose. Albert Schweitzer was a man who focused his entire career on the single idea of a reverence for life. Albert Einstein remarked that children ask simple and vital questions about space, time and life, and, thus, they show thinking people how to keep scientific inquiries uncomplicated. The genius of Einstein was characterized by qualities of wonder and simplicity of approach. Political and spiritual leader Mahatma Gandhi (1869-1948) lived humbly and sparingly, and advocated passive resistance in order to recover the rights of the lowest representatives of the social order in India.

Some of the most powerful leaders in the world have insisted upon directness and the absence of self-absorption. Pope John XXIII, who worked to bring peace among Catholics and Jews, wrote, "...I perceive the dignity and winning beauty of simplicity in thought, conduct and speech... ." He affirmed his "desire to treat everything with the greatest naturalness and clarity."[8]

Of course there have been some few valuable people in history who have seemed to lack "naturalness," and who have displayed more ego than modesty in their social contexts. Composer Richard Wagner was a fine example of a genius who lacked apparent reserve. However, the posturing of an egotistical person is quite often a disguise put on to hide some psycho-social weakness, and the ability to create masterpieces may even be developed for the very purpose of rising above a

---

[8] Pope John XXIII [Angelo Giuseppe Roncalli], *Journal of a Soul*, [New York: Doubleday, 1980].

sense of deep inferiority. Not all simple people will publicly confess their unpretentiousness, and some will pretend to be grandiose when they are not. What they create, artistically, will reveal the frankness of their secret selves. Certainly Wagner's inherent respect for a superior power is unveiled in his music.

Ultimately, humility and simplicity of character are alchemical ingredients that turn the efforts of remarkable individuals into an immortal legacy for future ages. Napoleon is known, but not honored; Stalin and Hitler are remembered, but dishonored. The good that some famous leaders do for their countries — (as with the welfare and public works campaigns of Stalin, Hitler and Eva Perón) — are based on self-interest, and are therefore exemplary of the natural balance of evil with good, rather than of the workings of great, creative minds. There is a force in the cosmos that permits positive effects to emanate from negative intentions.

Meanwhile, the greatest gains for all of humanity are made when unselfishness and creativity come together in the magic chemistry of production and invention. William Grant Still, himself described as a gentle and gentlemanly man, wrote,

> In Guy Endore's book, *King of Paris*, Alexandre Dumas is quoted as believing that the creators who really carve their names in history are the ones who write the serious, the difficult, the incomprehensible. "My works," he added, "are too easy. A child can read them. For this I will be forgotten."
>
> But he has not been forgotten, nor neglected. Neither have the simple, but profound teachings of Jesus been forgotten nor neglected. It may well be that there is a special virtue for posterity in presenting one's message in understandable terms.[9]

---

[9] Still, William Grant, "A Composer's Creed," *Music of the West* 17 [October 1961]; or, Spencer, Jon Michael, ed., *William Grant Still: A Reader* [Durham, North Carolina: Duke University Press, 1992] 200-201.

Cultivate Humility, Simplicity and Humor
Value a Sense of Humor

People are already beginning to regard him as a great man. He hears the things they say and is grateful for them, but he is never impressed with his own importance; At a meeting of the NAACP, after the speeches had been unusually long, someone noticed that the renowned composer, Mr. William Grant Still, was in the audience.[1] Would Mr. Still consent to speak to them on some matter of moment? The famed Mr. Still arose in an impressive silence. Then, with all eyes focused on him: "I wonder," said he quietly, "Whether everyone is as hungry as I am?" Then he sat down, and the meeting was dismissed.

- Verna Arvey[2]

William Grant Still had a whimsical sense of humor. Life was never happier for him than when he was playing and

---

[1] NAACP refers to the National Association for the Advancement of Colored People, one of the oldest and most influential civil rights organizations in the United States. The organization was founded in 1909.

[2] Arvey, *Studies*, 46.

49

laughing with his dogs, or children, or grandchildren. He sang nonsense syllables for the babies—"did'n, dad'n, dod'n," "bibbity-bobbity"—and finished with a chorus of "Frog Went a-Courtin'." Laughter strengthened him, and wit sparkled and danced in his music.

The greatest of public figures have had the grandest senses of humor. Verna Arvey not only chronicled the light moments in the life of William Grant Still, but she also recounted the stories of other famous people who were jokesters. She said that Franz Joseph Haydn was the author of "probably the most famous musical joke ever written," the "Surprise Symphony."[3] Frederic Chopin was the author of "comical pranks" to amuse his friends, imitating the King of Prussia, the Tsar, and other personalities. Rossini also did comic imitations of his employer Prinetti, and was fired therefore. Mozart had a child-like and ebullient love of fun, especially at parties.

Outside of the world of music, greatness and humor have always gone together. Benjamin Franklin, who never took himself too seriously, was the first to make light of his own part in embarrassing situations. At a dinner party in his honor, his stomach rumbled, and he announced, "Ladies and gentleman, apparently I have just swallowed a symphony orchestra.[4]

Abraham Lincoln was the quintessential quipster—he "joked more than any other President before or since."[5] At one point he described the Stephen Douglass' arguments for slavery as being, "as thin as a homeopathic soup that was

---

[3] Arvey, Verna, "When Great Musicians Were Boys," *Music World* 2, #4 [September 1931] 12.

[4] Cooke, "The Fabulous Doctor Franklin" Speech.

[5] Parshall, Gerald and Michael Barone, "Lincoln, To Those Who Knew Him," *U. S. News and World Report* [October 5, 1992].

made by boiling the shadow of a pigeon that had been starved to death.[6] Later, when colleagues told him that he should fire more than one member of his cabinet, he responded with the story of a farmer who set out to kill seven skunks. After the farmer killed one, "he raised such a fearful smell that I concluded it was best to let the other six go."[7]

While many of Lincoln's opponents and contemporaries did not take his joking as anything but a sign of a lightweight intelligence, later analysts have pointed out that President Lincoln used laughter, skillfully, to diffuse otherwise volatile situations. Great wit actually requires great genius, for it takes considerable insight to joke effectively with people of passionate political persuasions. Ted Cohen, Ph.D., of the University of Chicago explains that only one who understands people completely can be a successful humorist, since the response to a joke depends on the listener's ability to supply "the background required for the joke to succeed."[8]

Successful joking also reflects the healthy, life-affirming optimism that exceptional people have. Lincoln confessed, "I laugh because I must not weep," meaning that his humor was his weapon for change, and his defense against despair. Thomas Inge, an American writer on pop culture, has said that humor is helpful when, in politics, there is a great disparity between our ideals and our very egregious failures. When the reality of corruption does not match the values of life, liberty, equality and justice, we need someone like Mark Twain to declare, "There is no distinctly American criminal class except

---

[6] Quoted by Alonzo Rothschild in *Lincoln: Master of Men (A Study in Character)* [Boston: Houghton Mifflin, 1906].

[7] Parshall and Barone.

[8] Cohen, Ted, Ph.D., "Some Philosophical Thoughts About Jokes," *The Key Reporter* 66, #4 [Summer 2001] 4.

Congress."[9] In our time, humor, comedy and laughter are used more and more by physicians and psychologists as therapy for depression and illness.

Moreover, humor is a survival mechanism in life/death crises, and a strong force in the struggle for positive achievement. Researchers have learned that, among prisoners of war, those who tried to cultivate light-heartedness and high hopes for release, were more likely to live through the experience. They were also better suited for life after prison without serious psychological damage.[10] Those who are fatally ill and feel that they will get well, often do get well, while those who are pessimistic do not survive. Hope and humor mean endurance and accomplishment, in spite of any obstacles that must be overcome.

Above all, a good sense of humor, along with optimism, is a prime requisite for success in the commercial world, in the workplace and in society in general. Bennett Cerf (1898-1971), the much-admired co-founder of Random House publishing, pushed his company to the forefront by virtue of his affability and likeability. He was, reportedly, "always in good humor."[11] Media executive and advisor Roger Ailes (b. 1940) and communications trainer Jon Kraushar make the point that people who are not likable have a tendency in the workplace to cause personality conflicts, and they often lose their jobs even though they are intelligent and able.[12] Likable people become leaders in business and politics, as did John F.

---

9 Inge, M. Thomas, "Politics and the American Sense of Humor," *The Key Reporter* 71, #2 [Summer 2006] 8-9.

[10] Whitman, Ardis, "That Vital Spark—Hope," *Reader's Digest* 105, #631 [November 1974] 118.

[11] Ailes, Roger with Jon Kraushar, "The Importance of Being Likable," *Reader's Digest* 67 [May 1988] 133.

[12] Ailes, 134.

Kennedy and Ronald Reagan, while simply intelligent people, like Adlai Stevenson, are passed over.

Reagan, in fact, was another president whose rise to statesmanship was much-aided by his ability to make fun of himself. During a discourse on medical advances to an audience, he commented, "I've already lived some 23 years beyond my life-expectancy when I was born—and that's a source of great annoyance to a number of people."[13]

As William Grant Still said, laughing, when a newspaper reported that he had died years ago, "I'm so out of touch with public opinion, that I'm even the last to get the news of my own demise."

---

[13] Ailes, 135.

V

Expect, and Work Hard Against, Hardship
Expect Persecution

Praise God that I can accept adversity calmly, knowing that He will not suffer more to come than I can bear and that He will cause whatever comes to result eventually in good.

- William Grant Still[1]

William Grant Still endured, with enormous integrity and faith, the persecutions inflicted upon him because of his race, his genius and his ability to write non-traditional, yet melodic music. His first great opera, "Troubled Island," was panned by all of the East Coast critics. The racists reviled him, the mediocre composers demeaned him, the modernists called him "naïve." He might have said, as Abraham Lincoln did,

If I were to read, much less answer, all the attacks made on me, this shop might as well as be closed for any other business.[2]

---

[1] Still, William Grant, *Personal Journal*, "Praise," #117.

Suffering and persecution is, sadly, an almost inescapable aspect of human achievement. As Roman philosopher and dramatist Seneca (c4BC-65AD) commented, "It is a rough road that leads to the heights of greatness."[3] Philosopher Elbert Hubbard (1859-1915) expanded upon that theme thusly:

> The man who is anybody and who does anything is surely going to be criticized, vilified, and misunderstood. This is a part of the penalty for greatness, and every man understands it; and understands, too, that it is no proof of greatness. The final proof of greatness lies in being able to endure contumely without resentment.[4]

There is probably no genius who has not had to undergo tribulation, health challenges, oppositions of every sort. Many geniuses have been diseased, addicted to alcohol or drugs, or have had mental issues. Cultural historian Jacques Barzun made up a list of mad, degenerate, diseased or otherwise afflicted geniuses which included Torquato Tasso, Van Gogh, Sir Isaac Newton, Samuel Johnson, Emile Zola, Wagner, Henrik Ibsen and Tolstoy.[5]

---

[2] From a conversation in the White House, as reported by Francis B. Carpenter (1830-1900), who served as presidential portrait painter for six months during the Lincoln Administration, beginning in February 1864.

[3] Lucius Annaeus Seneca (the Younger), *Epistles*, Volume II, 84, 13.

[4] Hubbard, Elbert, "Get Out or Get in Line," *Love, Life and Work* [East Aurora, New York: Roycroft, 1906]; Elbert Hubbard was a renowned philosopher, author, editor and lecturer of the late 19th and early 20th centuries. In 1895, he founded the Roycrofters, a semi-communal community of artists and craftspeople, in East Aurora, New York. He and his wife were lost at sea, May 7, 1915, while traveling to England aboard the ill-fated Lusitania.

[5] Barzun, 345.

W. R. Bett also put together a catalog of "infirm" geniuses who had health or mental problems.[6] His list was on this order:

Thomas Carlyle – had untreatable mental conflicts.

Percy Bysshe Shelley – consumed laudanum.

Algernon Swinburne – was a drunk who suffered from fits.

Edgar Allan Poe – took alcohol and opium, was manic-depressive.

Thomas de Quincey – took opium.

Charles Pierre Baudelaire – became paralyzed, had syphilis.

Charles Lamb – was put in a strait jacket as a youth for mental difficulties.

Honoré de Balzac – suffered from hypertension.

John Keats – died of tuberculosis.

Robert Burns – had rheumatic fever.

Lord Byron – had a club foot.

Alexander Pope – was a hunchback, had headaches and asthma.

Many more notable persons than these have had health problems, and, in fact, William Grant Still suffered from bad teeth, headaches, dizziness and stomach trouble. But it is not a given that these problems were a side-effect of genius; if one investigates each case closely, it might well be seen that these personal difficulties were the result of the attempts of outsiders to destroy the careers and abilities of talented individuals.

---

[6] Bett, W. R., *The Infirmities of Genius* [New York: Philosophical Library, 1952].

Many of the physical afflictions of great persons are caused by poverty. Franz Schubert (1797-1828) was frequently without the funds to buy manuscript paper for composing. Giacomo Puccini (1858-1924) was employed as an organist in a small church after he failed in school, but he lost this job when he insinuated popular tunes into the church services.[7] So many composers, including William Grant Still, have been poorly paid, that Deems Taylor (1885-1966) was prompted to write an article called, "Most of Our Great Symphonies Were Written on Empty Stomachs."[8] "In fact," Taylor decided, "One of the attributes of genius, to my mind, is the possession of sufficient strength of character to persist in spite of neglect."[9]

The number of stellar composers, writers and artists who have dealt with poverty is so large that some artistic mentors tell those who want to create that they must abjure material rewards in order to do so. Modern-day songwriter William Knecht has stated, flatly, that no one creates with genius who desires fame, or wealth, or praise. The physical body does not count, insists Knecht—only the creation exists and has value.[10]

Yet, the troubles of great artists go beyond the financial arena. The creative genius often suffers from ridicule and rejection of a horrific kind, heaped upon him or her by shallow teachers, critics and employers who can not recognize, or equal, their worth. The work of a great person affects onlookers like a sudden burst of vernal air that intoxicates and uplifts, offering a sense of newness and movement, as well as solidity and permanence. Some are irritated by it: it reminds them that they are, in their actions

---

[7] Arvey, Verna, "When Great Musicians Were Boys," 12.

[8] Taylor, Deems, "Most of Our Great Symphonies Were Written on Empty Stomachs," *Up Beat* I [January 1939] 26.

[9] Taylor, 26.

[10] Knecht, William, "Creativity," *Songwriter's Monthly* [September 1993] 11.

and thoughts, falling short, and guilty of mediocrity. They set about to demean the artistic creations of the exceptional person, and to see that the public does not honor their expressions with undue attention. Beethoven was told by his instructor that he did not have a musical ear. Thomas Fleming, in *The Man Who Dared Lightening*, revealed that Benjamin Franklin was beset by criticism "even when the fate of the emerging United States hung in the balance," because "those who envied Franklin's gifts and accomplishments were quite willing to sacrifice the country to topple a titan."[11] Rudyard Kipling, Jack London and Margaret Mitchell received insensitive rejection letters from publishers, as have all of the best writers in the annals of literature. Abraham Lincoln, who authored the most magnificent orations in the history of American statesmanship, and whose "Gettysburg Address" was denigrated in the press, said, "I have endured a great deal of ridicule without much malice; and have received a great deal of kindness, not quite free from ridicule."[12]

In 1854, when Thomas Edison was ending his first three months of formal education, his teacher expelled him from school on the grounds of mental retardation. The 1,093 inventions that Edison later patented were 1,093 more than those attributable to his teacher. Charles Darwin (1809-1882) failed first-year algebra, and Einstein was criticized for his lower-than-average language abilities. He later responded to his critics with the statement that, "Great minds always encounter violent opposition from mediocre minds."

On a lower level of example, popular singer Bing Crosby (1903-1977) was not accepted into his college choir. Operatic

---

[11] Fleming, Thomas J., *The Man Who Dared Lightening: A New Look at Benjamin Franklin* [New York: Morrow Co., 1971].

[12] Lincoln, President Abraham, Letter to J. H. Hackett, November 2, 1863.

singer Marian Anderson (1897-1993) was advised by Carl Van Vechten (1880-1964), photographer and promoter of Negro talent during the Harlem Renaissance, that she could not be successful as a singer.[13]

On all levels of society, including the intellectual and professional level, genius is abused and rejected. As Ann Dirkes said of educational systems, the "inventions, art and ideas of outstanding individuals" are debunked, because "advanced discoveries and new ways of doing things are threats to many and nonsense to others."[14]

In 1935, Sir Arthur Eddington (1882-1944),[15] a world famous astronomer, humiliated the young Hindu scientist, Subrahmanyan Chandrasekhar (1910-1995),[16] by announcing that Chandrasekhar's theory of black holes was "absurd." Eddington's persecution of the young man prevented the latter from acquiring a tenured position in England, but he could not prevent the theory of black holes from obtaining the credence it deserved.[17]

Joseph Wood Krutch (1893-1970)[18] and educator Richard Goldman have deplored the fact that, in the universities,

---

[13] Van Vechten, Carl. Letter to Verna Arvey, September 13, 1943.

[14] Dirkes, 138.

[15] Sir Arthur Eddington was a prominent astrophysicist of his time who made several significant contributions to the area of physics. He was one of the first physicists who understood the early ideas of relativity along with Albert Einstein.

[16] Subrahmanyan Chandrasekhar was an Indian-American astrophysicist who is widely regarded as one of the foremost astrophysicists of the 20th century. His work proved to be crucial for the understanding of the spiral structure of galaxies. He earned a shared Nobel Prize in physics in 1983, and NASA's important X-ray observatory was named in his honor.

[17] Tierney, John, "Quest for Order," *Science 82*, 3, #7 [September 1982] 69-74.

[18] Joseph Wood Krutch was an American writer, critic and naturalist. He served as a theater critic for *The Nation*, and, he gained acclaim through his book, *The Modern Temper* (1929), a work critical of the impact of science and technology.

literary researchers and literary critics who are professors of literature, have attempted to control which writers become great and which will "endure" over time. These so-called experts have, in the past, praised the writings of Lew Wallace, Edmund Clarence Stedman, Bulwer Lyton, and yet these writers have not survived the decades. In the same way, critics praised Cervantes' *Persiles y Sigismunda*, instead of *Don Quixote*, and yet *Don Quixote* was a timeless treasure of literature, and *Persiles* was unreadable. In an earlier time, Twain's *Huckleberry Finn* was rejected as a "homosexual novel" by academic experts.[19] Richard Goldman warned researchers not to decide that literature was worthy according to prevailing fashions and reputation,[20] and Joseph Krutch denied, unconditionally, any influence of critics on the fate of literary works. Greatness, he said, is decided by virtue of itself, not according to its critics.[21]

While Krutch and Goldman were angry over the attempts of academicians to ignore works of genius, journalist and concert pianist Verna Arvey was pointing out the dangers of snobbery in the scholarly world. She suggested that a famous music magazine, *The Etude*, ultimately went out of print because it began to feature very avant-garde composers who wrote ugly music. These were composers, she said, like Copland, Bernstein and Roger Sessions, who "had managed to place themselves in positions of apparent prominence without having very much to say, musically speaking."[22]

---

[19] Krutch, Joseph Wood, "If You Don't Mind My Saying So...," *American Scholar* 36, #1 [Winter 1966-67] 14-17; Goldman, Richard Franko, "An X to the Left of the Writer," *American Scholar* 36, #1 [Winter 1966-67] 104-106.

[20] Goldman, 104.

[21] Krutch, 16.

[22] Arvey, Verna, "Death of the Etude," *Australian Musical News and Musical Digest* 49, #2 [August 1958].

The modernist composers who took control of *The Etude*, found that public opinion was more valuable than they were, and more lasting. They continued to attract notice for their music in the universities, academies and conservatories, and they campaigned to keep William Grant Still (and others) from obtaining interest in his works; but, even when music-lovers could not hear William Grant Still's music, it did not mean that audiences flocked to hear the unharmonious sounds of atonal composers.

The anti-melody campaign carried on by modernists who extolled "New Music," was unremitting during Still's life, nor did it end after William Grant Still died. As recently as 2005, a noted "expert" on concert music, Joseph Horowitz, suggested that the decline of classical music in America was due to a lack of focus on the post-modern composer. The European canon was programmed, over and above contemporary works of an "adventurous" nature. Horowitz lamented the decline of public support for American music, without noting that performances of the music of Still and of accessible composers were lovingly embraced by the populace once recordings of their music were made available. In the future, Horowitz and the exponents of "high culture," who are perplexed to see their opinions unvalidated by history, will be the last to admit that the struggles of Still to make a living in classical music were well worth making.[23]

And the good part was that Still's struggles made his creative efforts more passionate and impressive, and when the music was finally heard on recordings, it was the more memorable. As greatness develops in those who strive against enormous odds, the incandescence of expression increases in

---

[23] Horowitz, Joseph. *Classical Music in America: A History of Its Rise and Fall* [New York: W. W. Morton, 2005].

direct ratio to the hardships encountered. Great people do not just suffer, they create while suffering. If one pounds wood with a hammer in an indifferent manner, the marks on the wood will be slight; however, if the pounding is heavy, the indentation will be deep.

Hector Berlioz (1803-1869) wrote his most creative pieces of music when he was lovelorn, as, for instance, "The Symphony Fantastik." Negro spirituals are compellingly beautiful because they are distilled by the hardships caused by bigotry, and, as one observer indicates, they are full of the melancholy and the grave, and the "notes which appear to be hushed in a sob and in the translation of a people through its history of suffering and slavery."[24]

The spirituals show us that even the severest kind of penury can be turned from the negative into a positive by human creativity and faith. It is not necessary for poverty and travail to destroy men's lives. The lack of material means does, in actuality, produce some beneficial dividends. In the Negro communities right after slavery, and in Europe today where the standard of living is low, elderly family members must often live with their children after the death of a spouse. Children grow up, then, benefiting from the presence of a wise, experienced grandparent in their lives. In the United States today, however, in families of means, the older folk more often live alone, or in retirement homes, without reward to themselves or to other relatives. Moreover, among people of good will, having too little where others also have few resources, frequently encourages real appreciation for the small, rich gifts of nature and of emotion.

---

[24] Moses, Rudolph, "A Modern Odyssey," *Arts Quarterly* [October-December 1937] 22-23.

Most importantly, the lack of luxury and material clutter in a valuable person's life causes him or her to create his or her own intellectual and emotional world of value. On December 5, 1932, an unknown writer commented to William Grant Still in a private letter, "Elmer Rice says—as many another has felt—that an artist is an unhappy man who compensates through art. ...In fact doesn't the world of disillusioning reality and the severity of the day by day living force the artist to do his best work?"

So it is that great artists suffer and create, create and suffer. Their resultant creations are scorned, and they themselves are slandered and poorly recompensed. Yet, the work that they do retains its inestimable merit and truth, and, as President Abraham Lincoln promised, "Truth is generally the best vindication against slander."[25] Even if great people are not slandered, they are almost always faced with hardships. Polish-French chemist Marie Curie (1867-1934), the discoverer of radium, overcame many obstacles, because, she said, "...we must persevere and have confidence in ourselves. We must believe that our gifts were given to us for some purpose, and we must attain to that purpose, whatever the price we have to pay for it." And, in the words of William Grant Still, an artist may often have "not enough to eat," and may find himself "working harder" as the problems grow harder, but "I firmly believe that if [he] has faith in himself, and sticks to his convictions—even to the point of being willing to starve for them, if need be—he will triumph in the end."[26]

---

[25] Lincoln, President Abraham. Letter to Secretary Stanton, July 18, 1864.
[26] Still, "The Composer Needs Determination and Faith," 8.

Expect, and Work
Hard Against, Hardship
Work Hard and Long

I compose with pain I enjoy.

- William Grant Still[1]

Certainly people who are marked for greatness arrive on the planet in infancy with all of the tools that they need to tune into the creative voice of the cosmos, and to shape experience, emotion and inspiration into eternal monuments to themselves and to humanity. But let no one think that the shaping and the sculpting are easy. Genius, says Jacques Barzun, is "sudden illumination" plus "unwearied persistence."[2]

Almost all biographers of famous people have agreed that achievement requires much labor and concentration. In telling about the compositional approach of Mozart, modern-day

---

[1] Reno, Doris, "I Compose With Pain I Enjoy," *Miami Herald*, Section E19, October 29, 1961.
[2] Barzun, 346.

composer Michael Colgrass (b. 1932) said that Mozart's genius came from "very hard work and the development of an enormous amount of skill," experience, and the acquisition of knowledge.

> Mozart had a great gift, and maybe even a direct line to supernatural powers, but he also worked prodigiously and absorbed the knowledge and practices of the great composers who preceded him.[3]

Johann Sebastian Bach said, "Oh, anyone could do as I have done [with music], if he only worked as hard as I do."[4] Clara Wieck (1819-1896), the wife of composer Robert Schumann (1810-1856), became a fine pianist because her father insisted that she practice for extended periods every day.[5] Charles Dickens (1812-1870) spent long mornings with many unsuccessful starts to his writings in order to produce fifteen novels, and other works.

Skill gives us choices in the matter of creation, while rationality and constructive effort enter into the building process of every creative artifact. The good writer or composer rewrites, crosses out passages, adds new ideas, revises and discards many inferior drafts. Imperial Court Composer Antonio Salieri (1750-1825) was lazy, and settled for a mediocre product. Beethoven (1770-1827) rewrote his "Ode to Joy" 200 times until he had the version that pleased him. Also, Beethoven's second movement of his "Fifth Symphony" was built on a theme of thirty-two notes which he revised fourteen times in eight years.[6]

---

[3] Colgrass, Michael, "Speaking of Music: The Real Mystery of Salieri," *Music Magazine* 8 [January-February 1985] 38.

[4] Arvey, "When Great Musicians Were Boys," 12.

[5] Arvey, "When Great Musicians Were Boys," 13.

[6] Colgrass, 38.

Quite often, according to Barzun, the true artist goes through long periods of time when he or she can set down nothing that is valuable. French novelist Honoré de Balzac (1799-1850) produced ten years of unremarkable literature, writing and rewriting, until he came up with his masterwork, *The Human Comedy*.[7] American writer Herman Melville (1819-1891), in my estimation, only wrote one great work: *Moby Dick*.

Yet the creative artist, whether he or she produces one significant work or dozens, is the only one who can play host to that triumph. Each aspiring individual must take charge of his or her fate, making a conscious effort to rise above the periods of mental drought (and the long hours of indecision and awkward stumbling) to bring forth a timeless and superior invention. One who does not sign on for a seemingly endless, grueling voyage, will not reach the chosen destination.

Even those who are not truly great have recognized the need for protracted labor in the aspiration toward greatness. President Theodore Roosevelt (1858-1919), a man with many frailties (which included racial bigotry), was nevertheless the source of a magnificent statement about the need for arduous effort in the pursuit of achievement. He said:

The Battle of Life

It is not the critic who counts, nor the man who points out how the strong man stumbles or where the doer of deeds could have done better. The credit belongs to the man who is actually in the arena; whose face is marred with dust and sweat; who strives valiantly; who errs and may fall again and again, because there is not effort without error or shortcoming, but who does actually strive

---

[7] Barzun, 346.

to do the deeds; who does know the great enthusiasm, the great devotion; who spends himself in a worthy cause; who at best knows in the end the triumph of high achievement and who at the worst, if he fails, at least fails while daring greatly, so that his place shall never be with those cold or timid souls who know neither victory nor defeat.[8]

It would be difficult to find a truly notable and reverend figure in history who did not toil unceasingly to become notable. Benjamin Franklin, as a young printer in Philadelphia, was often observed in the early morning pushing wheelbarrows of paper from the papermaker to his shop for his daily use. He worked late into the evening, then went to his room to study philosophy, science and the five languages of which he gained command. Thomas Edison and his assistants spent 60 hours at a time researching particular problems, and it was Edison who declared, "Genius is 1% inspiration and 99% perspiration." American poet Henry Wadsworth Longfellow (1807-1882) uttered the same sentiment when he wrote,

> The heights by great men reached and kept
> Were not attained by sudden flight,
> But they, while their companions slept,
> Were toiling upward in the night.[9]

Helen Keller (1880-1968), overcame deafness and blindness, and graduated Cum Laude from Radcliffe College in Cambridge, Massachusetts, obtaining her degree with no special help from outside sources. Between 1902 and 1968, she

---

[8] Roosevelt, Theodore, "Citizenship in a Republic," Speech at the Sorbonne, Paris, April 23, 1910.

[9] Peterson, Dennis L., "Help Wanted: Laborers," *The Freeman* 31, #5 [May 1981] 287.

wrote many inspiring books and articles.[10] Charles Schulz (1922-2000) whose "Peanuts" cartoons delighted millions, worked so energetically in school that he filled whole sheets with unusual drawings, even when he was asked to draw only three objects. Bobby McFerrin (b. 1950), renowned African-American singer, composer and conductor, told an interviewer that, "The ratio between reading and studying to creating is anywhere from four-to-one to five-to-one."[11]

In all of the manifestations of greatness at work, the final product—whether it be a sculpture, a painting, a book, a poem, or a piece of music—is reached after much effort is expended. A creative masterpiece may begin with a flash of insight, but it is developed only through the methodical application of demanding principles of construction. Creation is a step-by-step process which refines the raw materials of experience, knowledge and aesthetic taste. As psychologist Albert Rothenberg indicates, in discussing the authorship of the finest poems, the study of great poems from first draft to the final, publishable manuscript shows that "the free driving quality of good poems is arduously achieved, not born in one piece."[12] Edgar Allan Poe (1809-1849), says Rothenberg, built his poems in the architectural manner, revising continuously and laboring over each development.

In music, a similar compositional process has been described by renown psychiatrist Silvano Arieti (1914-1981).[13] Arieti explains that a composer receives a melodic idea (an

---

[10] Keller, Helen. *The Story of My Life* [New York: Dell Publishing Co., 1972].

[11] Editorial, Interviews with Creative People, "The Creators," 42.

[12] Rothenberg, Albert, "Inspiration, Insight and the Creative Process in Poetry," *College English* 32, #2 [November 1970] 174.

[13] Arieti, Silvano. *Creativity: The Magic Synthesis* [New York: Basic Books, Inc., 1976].

"acoustic phrase") from "an external source." The composer then develops the idea into a construct, or form, in the same way that an architect plans the basic structure of a building. The composer makes choices as to how to develop the form in a way that expresses its nature appropriately; these choices are made according to the composer's own musical environment of experience and aesthetic taste.[14]

William Grant Still's way of composing, as outlined in his diaries, revealed a similar approach to musical creation. He began every work by getting the theme from a spiritual source, then he planned the structure of the piece logically and consciously. He wrote about eight measures every day, between 8:00 a.m. and noon, working his way from beginning to end, expressing the theme in an accretionary fashion. He rewrote, improved, or threw out a day's work if it seemed not to fit into his conception of form and content. When conductors, musicians and critics tried to convince him to change his conception to fit their predilections, he was polite but sure of himself; he relied on his own sense of correctness to sustain him against outside pressures. No one influenced him in matters that required compositional skill. In his journal, he wrote:

Truth: Accomplishment is the sum of desire and effort.[15]

Truth: Education is desirable, but the high road of experience leadeth not unto error.[16]

Later, when Still was in his 70's, he was still composing, and he repeated to an interviewer his idea that creativity was

---

[14] Arieti, 239.

[15] Still, William Grant. *Personal Journal*, "Truth," #110.

[16] Still, William Grant. *Personal Journal*, "Truth," #111.

work, and more work than teaching or reviewing: artists, he said, put things together, while teachers and critics merely take them apart for analysis.[17]

Not only did the composer labor diligently with his music, but also he spent many hours trying to develop a sense of the skills required in other areas of expertise. He worked in carpentry, drawing, writing, oratory, and even in sculpting and carving. In his diary on April 20, 1950, he wrote, "Trying to carve a head just to be able to grasp the principle involved." Still dabbled in these fields just to improve his understanding and breadth of experience, but he did not overspend his time and energy hoping to excel in skills that were not in his life-plan. He was more than realistic about his proper occupation.

The admonition should be made, therefore, against attempting to be first in every line in a life-time. There are people who want to excel at everything, even at skills of which they have no grasp. They waste time and money trying to develop talents which they will never have, and, in the process, do not use their real strengths to the extent that aptitude and potential will permit.

I have personally known three people, a man and two women, who have missed their appointments with destiny for the reason that they wanted to be, and were not, great singers on the concert stage. One young girl was a fine performer in musical comedies, who had a flair for playing the comic relief in popular entertainments. She, however, aspired to be a diva in grand opera, in which pursuit she failed miserably. Ultimately she ended her career on the streets, and then in jail. Her young son was placed in foster care.

---

[17] Brown, 41-42.

Another lady was a successful shop owner and spokesperson for charitable and social causes. She was a forceful speaker and promoter of community events, as well as a person of great inner beauty. She was loved by all. The one thing that she could not do was to sing, and that is the one thing that she persisted in wanting to do. She arranged concerts and attended musical symposia so that she could perform, yet she never seemed to realize how the hearts of her audiences sank when they heard her. Had she continued to hone her skills as a speaker and promoter, what rich gifts she could have given to the people of her city.

A third person, a man who had a fair career as a singer, and who even played a bit part in a popular Hollywood film, was intent upon national recognition. It was his notion that, to accept any less than leading roles and top dollar for his engagements, was demeaning. The result was that he spent most of his career living off the largesse of women and men who believed in his assessment of himself. He ruined his health with alcohol and poor eating habits, and up until the year of his death from overindulgence, he busied himself begging money from friends and making passes at well-fixed females.

Gifted people and intelligent people may have singular abilities, but they do not do singular things in life unless they recognize their strengths and ignore their weaknesses. The human Will determines which geniuses and which talented people will become great. The persons who are great and powerful, both, are the persons who allow others to shine in the feats which are beyond them, nor are they jealous and spiteful when others reach heights to which they can not aspire. Not everyone can be a movie personality, or an operatic diva, nor do all such divas and stars outlast the generations in true achievement.

The one variable that makes for success unto the generations, once one has accepted the appropriate path in life, is hard work. The importance of hard work in the lives of all humans, whether creative or banal, high-born or low-born, fortunate or unfortunate, was aptly discussed by Abraham Lincoln, in a letter to his rather unambitious stepbrother, John D. Johnston, on December 24, 1848:

Dear Johnston:

Your request for eighty dollars I do not think it best to comply with now. At the various times when I have helped you a little, you have said to me, "We can get along very well now," but in a very short time I find you in the same difficulty again. Now this can only happen by some defect in your conduct. What that defect is, I think I know. You are not lazy, and still you are an idler. I doubt whether since I saw you, you have done a good whole day's work, in any one day. You do not very much dislike to work; and still you do not work much, merely because it does not seem to you that you could get much for it. This habit of needlessly wasting time, is the whole difficulty; and it is vastly important to you, and still more so to your children, that you should break this habit. It is more important to them, because they have longer to live, and can keep out of an idle habit before they are in it, easier than they can get out after they are in. ...What I propose is, that you shall go to work, "tooth and nails," for somebody who will give you money for it.

Daily practice, extended days, total commitment to the God-given life-activity—these alone sustain and reward the pursuit of greatness.[18] As Michael Hurd put it, a work of art is "a distillation of long hours of thought and imagination."[19] Or, as Verna Arvey said, regarding composer Still's

---

[18] Clifton, Donald O. and Paula Nelson, *Soar With Your Strength* [New York: Dell Publishing Company, 1992].

[19] Francis, 7.

"absorption in work," his constant interest in his composing "wasn't a pose:"

Still has few recreations. He is not a "social" person. Almost all of his time is spent in steady, feverish work, in an effort to get everything done, to say all he must say before it is too late. One afternoon a visitor entered. "It's so warm today!" he remarked.

Still looked up from his composing. "Is it?" he asked.
"Yes."
"Then I guess I'd better take off my coat."[20]

---

[20] Arvey, *Studies*, 45-46.

VI

Use Nature's Rhythms in Creation

My feeling is that a composer should be tested, not by the bizarre sounds he can produce, but by his ability to construct a simple, satisfying piece of music, harmonically, melodically and architecturally.

- William Grant Still[1]

Good music must follow God-given rules of order. A good musical composition must have a pleasing melody, form, variety and harmonic treatment using conventional harmonies.

- William Grant Still[2]

"God's voice" is "an elegant melody," i.e. God's voice is heard in music.

- William Grant Still[3]

---

[1] Still, William Grant, "The Structure of Music," *William Grant Still: A Reader*, Jon Michael Spencer, ed. [Durham, North Carolina: Duke University Press, 1992] 176.

[2] Still, William Grant. Summary of a letter to Miss Rose Heylbut, August 29, 1948.

[3] Still, William Grant. *Personal Journal*, "Praise."

Music is the language of the spirit. It opens the secret of
life, bringing peace, abolishing strife.

- Khalil Gibran[4]

William Grant Still believed that form follows function,
and that composing was a part of the natural order of the
universe. His belief was so intrinsic to his music that his
hearers often perceived it simply from listening to his works.
On December 5, 1932, a fan wrote to the composer that he
wondered "whether subject matter for a work of art doesn't
inevitably pour itself out in its own form when sounded
deeply."

The music of Still, and of Puccini, Bach, Beethoven,
Mozart, and of other fine composers, constitutes a probing of
the mystery of existence. The great creative genius is keenly
receptive to the power of the cosmos and to the force of
destiny, and like primitive humans in tribal communities, the
artistic individual works in accordance with nature. The great
person has a sense of wonder at the glories of the natural
order. Einstein, in particular, expressed his awe of the
harmony of natural law and causality.[5]

The artist, says writer Arthur Koestler (1905-1983), attempts
to capture the oceanic feeling—the concept of "oneness with
the universe"—"on a higher level of development—at a
higher turn of the spiral."[6] In fact, creativity which is "at a
higher turn of the spiral," can be compared to the process of
photosynthesis, wherein sunlight engenders the production of
chlorophyll in vegetation. English poet John Milton (1608-
1674) in his epic poem, "Paradise Lost," revealed his awe of

---

[4] Gibran, Khalil. *The Prophet* [New York: Alfred A. Knopf, Inc. 1923].

[5] Einstein, Albert. *The World As I See It* [New York: Carol Publishing
Group, 1991].

[6] Koestler, 293.

the heavenly bodies—("Hail, holy light!" Book III, line 1)—and his wonder at the magnificence of the universe.[7] After looking through Galileo's telescope, Milton described outer space as "a dark illimitable ocean, without bound, Without dimension."[8]

The feeling of oneness with a limitless immensity is not the only quality that ties the creative human being to the cosmos. There is also a tremendous apprehension of the diversity in nature, the unending proliferation of differences on earth and in space. Indeed, in all of existence there is a paradoxical interplay of variety plus wholeness. The universe unites, through an all-powerful system of balances and harmonies, disparate objects and individuals. Separate and unique persons are contained by an unerring complex of form, yet they are separate from each other enough to allow freedom to pursue varying goals and purposes. Disharmony and self-interest are permitted, with the understanding that they will always be balanced by order and harmony of effort. Human creativity requires the ability to recognize the potential harmony in dissimilar things, and to favor harmony over disharmony.

Perhaps the reason that so many great men and women become musicians is that life is rather like musical orchestration—the blending of varying tones and treatments to create a harmonious whole. Phenomena in nature have form, rhythm, harmony and the other attributes of a musical composition, to the extent that Bobby McFerrin called music, "the scent of the rose."[9] E. E. Kidder-Smith, in speaking of the creative genius of Thomas Jefferson, characterized Jefferson's

---

[7] Milton, John, "Paradise Lost," 1667.
[8] Koestler, 674.
[9] Editorial, Interviews with Creative People, "The Creators," 42.

creative accomplishments in his home at Monticello as "excitement plus order."[10]

Also within the ordered harmonies of life and of music, there are levels of sophistication and opportunities for evolution of taste. A small child is primarily attuned to simple melodies and nursery rhymes, and his or her attunement is simple, balanced and complete. The teenager may be open to more complex and dissonant sounds, plus the emotional conflicts that come with adolescence can be reflected in teenage musical tastes. Mature individuals will gravitate toward more profound, peaceful or stately musical entertainment. People with mental and emotional problems may listen to loud and jarring noises (erroneously called music), while misguided proponents of avant garde art and music retard artistic development by promoting disharmony.

One of the problems in the arts and music in the 20th century was the overuse of formlessness, disharmony and dissonance by American composers, artists and authors. After the first World War, intellectuals decided that global affairs were steeped in discord and evil, and any expression of life and culture had likewise to be discordant. From 1920 to the present, the public has been regaled with atonal music, avant-garde art, shapeless sculptures, to the extent that all of existence has the aura of disruption and incoherence. The result of the overemphasis on the harsh and the ugly in our culture, has been a decline in creative ability and in mental health of the populace.

Spiritual teachers tell us that art, music and literature act upon the nervous systems of humans, because the vibrations of molecules in the body are affected by sounds and visual

---

[10] Kidder-Smith, E. E. KCET-PBS Television, Channel 28, Los Angeles, California [August 2, 1978] 9:00 p.m.

and verbal rhythms. The nervous system of an individual must be able to communicate the sound of music that is heard to the cells of the body, but too much harsh sound can upset the nervous system so much that ill health results. Harmony and dissonance together, in great music, create movement, yet unresolved dissonances leave audiences with a sense of futility and irritation. Tonal music heals, discord destroys equilibrium. The spiritual light-forces, known as The WWs, stated this:

> ...It will soon be scientifically proven that disharmonic music has a detrimental effect on the bodily functions of humans. ...The action of the tones in juxtaposition with each other act on the human organism. The nervous system must be able to communicate the sound. The effect is on the nervous system, which of course is a communication system, and which then gives less work only to the cells it serves. The disharmony, if not prolonged, may be very useful in some respects. But to prolong such music or sounds does have disintegrating power." (12/31/57) [11]

Fortunately, the laws of harmony will eventually prevail in the arts as they do in nature. Musicians and artists who create displeasing works, often insisting that they have a right to their own forms of expression, will find themselves unregarded as the Millennium advances. A resolution to do what one pleases, regardless of its detrimental effects for others, will not be allowed to go unchecked interminably in the scheme of things. Self-interest, unresolved disharmony, and ugliness in the creative arts are all aspects of cosmic darkness and evil, for evil is the pursuit of unmitigated self-glorification. On the other hand, goodness and greatness are

---

[11] Judith Anne Still, "The WWs and World Visions," [Flagstaff, AZ: The Master-Player Library, publication pending].

the perfect balance of self-interest with concern for others, or, the delicate harmonization of self-esteem and individual initiative with reverence for the whole.

Throughout history, eras of darkness in human activity have habitually been followed by periods of enlightenment. The ancient Egyptians, with their vast understanding of astronomy, geometry and the mystic arts, were followed by barbaric rule in Egypt. The philosophic Greeks were superseded by the insensitive and ruthless Romans. The Dark Ages and Middle Ages in Europe gave way, inexorably, to the Renaissance and, later, to the Enlightenment. All light gives way to darkness, darkness to light. No matter the depths of disorder, this, too, shall pass away. The growing interest in the music of William Grant Still reveals the coming end to the period of formless, unharmonious art and music in America.

In order to facilitate the understanding that will undergird the new age of cultural enrichment that is entering apace, it is well to look at some of the ways in which great art, music and literature exemplify the same principles as those which are invested in the natural order of the earth. The first point of comparison between nature and art is in the area of mathematics: both the Universal Creator and the human creator put order into disorder through the numerical patterns. In music, in verbiage, in architecture, and in all other cultural expressions, rhythmic patterns carry meaning and provide structure and form. In the human body, and in all other material entities, molecules vibrate in rhythmic and melodic patterns that can be described mathematically, to the extent that Pythagoreans pictured the universe as a large "musical box," and all material phenomena as "a dance of numbers."[12]

---

[12] Koestler, 313.

That everything in nature and in art is related numerically to everything else, is dimly realized when one learns certain mathematical tricks that can be performed by anyone. For example, when one multiples a number by 9, the digits in the answer will always total 9, or a multiple of 9. And, to find out how many years it takes for money to double at compound interest, one must divide 70 by the interest rate. In other words, at 6% interest, the money will double in 12 years. Also, the mathematical proportions of the body are all perfectly related to each other. My father taught me, as the ancient wisdom was passed on to him, that, in God's perfectly proportioned world, a person can tell whether socks are the correct size for the feet by winding the socks around the fist.

The intricately computable relationships in nature and art exist whether humans are consciously aware of them, or not. In nature, thorns and roses can combine attractively, though they contrast with each other in aspect. The true creative genius intuits their reality, and expresses that reality, even if, superficially and unimaginatively, elements that are juxtaposed seem to be unlike each other. The creative mind explores, not the superficial images of pop art, but relationships between dissimilar things, as in the comparisons, or "conceits," of the metaphysical poets such as John Donne (1573-1631).

For example, Donne, in his "Valediction, Forbidding Mourning," compared two people who shared an intimate relationship with each other to "twin compasses."[13] In his most famous "Meditation XVII," Donne described the solitary human being as "a peece of the Continent, a part of the main;" for "No man is an Island, intire of itself... ."[14] The poet

---

[13] Donne, John, "Valediction, Forbidding Mourning," 1611.
[14] Donne, John, "Meditation XVII," 1624.

explained his combinations of unlikely comparisons by indicating that there is order in the world "beyond our power to grasp," and that the truth of that order "is in the great images which lie behind."[15]

Other poets like Donne also used metaphors effectively to express the metaphysical interrelatedness of material objects and creatures. Richard Crashaw (1613-1649), in "Saint Mary Magdalene," described eyes as "fountains," "baths" and "portable oceans."[16] John Milton called outer space "the wide womb of uncreated night,"[17] and evening "a sad votarist in palmer's weed."[18]

Long before Donne, Milton and Crashaw, Aristotle (384-322 B.C.) recommended the use of metaphors to poets, asserting that the "sign of genius" is to be able to make artistic employment of metaphor, according to the "intuitive perception of the similarity in the dissimilar."[19] Arieti, in discussing Aristotle's dictum, observed that the person who suffers from schizophrenia substitutes one dissimilar object for another in his or her mind, as a normal person does while dreaming. The difference between a schizophrenic and a poet is that the latter merely compares unlike objects without believing that one becomes another.[20] Arieti went on to suggest that, in the greatest works of art and literature, more than one metaphor and level of meaning are present. Each is unique, each produces pleasure, and all are combined in a satisfying unity of form. Thus, metaphor is the most

---

[15] Eiseley, Loren, "The Illusion of Two Cultures," Speech for the Richard Prentice Ettinger Program for Creative Writing [New York: Rockefeller Institute, October 29, 1963] 395-396.

[16] Crashaw, Richard, "Saint Mary Magdalene, or The Weeper," 1646.

[17] Milton, John, "Paradise Lost," 1667.

[18] Milton, John, "Comus," 1634.

[19] Aristotle, *Poetics*, 350 B.C.

[20] Arieti, 137.

immediate aspect of creative genius, for it deepens our understanding of the possibilities in the cosmos.[21]

Understanding comes because metaphor is actually a replication of the diversity in nature, and a glimpse of the vastness of cosmic variability. In pictorial art, painters and illustrators graphically compare the beauties of the human body to natural wonders, goodness to light, death to evening, life to springtime abundance. The master painter is so-called because he or she sees and objectifies the blue and white and violet on a tree trunk, while the novice artist sees only a brown column. Children draw trees as straight brown sticks with round green balls on top. As they grow up, they begin to be cognizant of variety and gradation of form, and of nuances of color. If they become artists, they learn to enhance the nuances and sophistication of their pictures, as they manipulate perspective and the juxtaposition of objects to convey subtle meanings.

An additional layer of variability in nature and in creative efforts comes when the life-experiences and perceptions of artists blend with the multiplicities of observed reality. Reality is a constant, to the extent that it is not haphazard or free from natural laws, but our assessment of reality clothes the world's absolutes in various costumes taken from a gorgeous wardrobe of differences, nuances and colorful memories. Memories waft around the reality like the ephemera of longing ghosts—near the truth, but altered by shifting perceptions and experiences. A cabin in the summer moonlight looks totally different from the same cabin in the snow, or in the rust of autumn, or in the bursting dawn of a spring morning. The world for the Middle Ages was different,

---

[21] Arieti, 144.

culturally and politically, from the world of today, because pre-Renaissance society perceived the earth as the center of the solar system, and believed that the sun revolved around the earth. This perception directed human affairs, in spite of the reality. In the Civil War, President Lincoln was a different man to the North, than he was to the South. To a General, war is a noble occupation; to a pacifist, war is hell. Moreover, changing attitudes can alter perceptions of each onlooker of a situation: at some moment in his career, the General may decide that war is hell, while the pacifist decides to defend his or her ideals with physical force.

To the artist, differences in perception are blended with the highest of spiritual goals in every point of view, to create an artistic product that is appealing to people in all walks of life. Lovers of great art respond to the universality in creativity, for real artistry harmonizes constancy and uniqueness with variability and personal charm.

Whatever the medium of communication preferred by lovers of art, music and literature, the same fundamentals of variety, contrast, unity and balance pertain. Like the spider building a perfectly constructed web which will be his home, the design of an artist will be architecturally and mathematically consistent, balanced, and exquisite in form and pattern. Form is the rational organization of elements, and the form defines the function of a work of art. In music, form is linear, and develops "logically and naturally" from one point to another. Musical themes are developed in patterns, and melodies and countermelodies are not allowed to "obstruct" each other.[22] It is only through the logic of the

---

[22] Reed, Alfred, "How a Composer Works," *The Instrumentalist* 44, #11 [June 1990] 48-49.

patterns and forms that the artist has "any chance of being understood by his readers or listeners."[23]

The relation of form and pattern to appreciation of artistic masterpieces becomes clear when we realize that scientists like Albert Einstein were devoted fans of composers such as Mozart. Einstein might also have praised some of the compositions of William Grant Still, for, like Mozart, Still succeeded in interpreting the universe in an ordered fashion, at a higher turn of the spiral. An admirer of Still's expressed the composer's level of accomplishment when he wrote,

> Your style seems to reach a very delicate balance, with wild rhythms and also warm melody—it still makes demands on the performer and the listener—it is not "destructive" music. Today we live in harsh, dissonant times—but in your music, I feel a type of re-birth—warmth, love, compassion,—along with death and tragedy. ...But...maybe the feelings, the power we receive from your music is...just beauty.
>
> - Bradley Parker-Faye[24]

---

[23] Reed, 48.

[24] Parker-Faye, Bradley. Letter to William Grant Still [September 25, 1974].

VII

Tap into the Higher Power

God is my inspiration.

- William Grant Still[1]

Truth: What is creative ability? Some may say, "Experience plus originality, losing sight of the fact that originality is creative power. The answer is simple, for creative ability is a special gift coming from without, and it is the hand of God that bestows it."

- William Grant Still[2]

O Lord, how great are thy works: and thy thoughts are
    very deep.
A brutish man knoweth not; neither doth a fool understand
    this.

- *The Bible*, Old Testament, Psalm 92:56

I am careful not to confuse excellence with perfection. Excellence, I can reach for; perfection is God's business.

- Actor Michael J. Fox

---

[1] Still, William Grant. Inscription in Dr. Theodore Baker's *A Dictionary of Musical Terms*, [New York : G. Schirmer, 1906].

[2] Still, William Grant. *Personal Journal*, "Truth," #103.

It is a wonder to me that so many highly intelligent people have huge senses of ownership. A person with a high IQ may very well harbor a large ego, and the idea that he or she knows all that is worth knowing. Many smart people feel, subconsciously, that they are smart because they deserve to be above the norm.

The irony of ego in high IQ people is that, all too often, those with superior minds and enormous egos do not accomplish much in life. They may gain money, or power, or even transitory fame, but they do not achieve substantive greatness where history and culture are concerned. The problem is that these intellectual "giants" do not treat their gifts as blessings from a higher source that are given to them for a lofty, universal purpose. It does not occur to them that, because they did not create themselves, nor can they create biological life of their own doing, the talent that they possess is not really theirs. They must either use it to enhance the lives of others, or they will lose it after the soul leaves the body behind.

Helen Wambach, Ph.D., a psychologist who has research- ed the existence of the soul before birth, tells us that we are not here on the earth to feed our self-interests; we do not come into human bodies to acquire wealth, or status—we come to relate to others on a giving level. Karma is the obligation to use any of our personal gifts to help others, not to harm anyone. If this obligation is not met, it must be met in future incarnations, with or without IQ or talent.[3]

Although the majority of people do believe in the immortality of the soul, they balk at the concept of reincarnation. However, scientific investigations are moving

---

[3] Wambach, Helen, Ph.D. *Life Before Life* [New York: Bantam Books, 1979] 90.

ever and ever closer to a spiritual explanation for creative genius, and to the idea that genius is one aspect of the progress of the soul toward an invisible, ineffable goal.

At one time, philosophers like John Locke (1632-1704) believed that human beings began life with no creative abilities. The mind was thought to be a "tabula rasa" — a blank tablet that would be populated with sensory experiences. It was not known how the growing child acquired the creative skills to order experiences in the contexts of art, music and literature.

As time went on, researchers discovered that, scientifically speaking, it is impossible to create something out of nothing. The law of conservation of energy and matter affirms that all creativity in the cosmos is a transformation of a pre-existing thing.[4] Even a vacuum is not empty; it contains "quantum fluctuations" which can "coagulate into something."[5]

These laws of conservation of matter were first clearly formulated by Benjamin Franklin, who was perhaps the first American scientist to believe in the immortality of the soul, in the existence of the soul in another environment after death, and, by extension, in reincarnation. Franklin said,

> The power of man relative to matter seems limited to the dividing it, or mixing the various kinds of it, or changing its form and appearance by differing compositions of it, but does not extend to the making or creating of new matter, or annihilating the old.
>
> I say that when I see nothing annihilated, and not even a drop of water wasted, I cannot suspect the annihilation of souls, or believe that he will suffer the daily waste of millions of minds ready made that now exist, and put himself to the continual trouble of making new ones.

---

[4] Barzun, 337.
[5] Barzun, 338.

Thus finding myself to exist in the world, I believe I shall, in some shape or other, always exist.[6]

Franklin believed so strongly that the soul carried on through time, that his epitaph, written by himself declared the following:

The Body
Of
BENJAMIN FRANKLIN
Printer
(Like the Cover of an Old Book
Its Contents Torn Out
And Stript of its Lettering and Gilding)
Lies Here, Food for Worms.
But the Work Shall Not Be Lost
For It Will (As He Believed) Appear Once More
In a New and More Elegant Edition
Revised and Corrected
By
The Author

Other scientists, as, for example, Newton, Hertz, Maxwell, Faraday, Boyle, Mendeleyev, van't Hoff, Michelson, Planck, Bell, Edison and Einstein, amplified Franklin's beliefs by working with "invisible reality:" They indicated that 99% of reality is invisible; there is nothing solid or static in the universe. Everything consists of wave-frequencies and quanta events that are weighable, but not visible.[7]

This knowledge about the pervasiveness and power of electromagnetic energy, was later augmented by discoveries about DNA and RNA. The realization that all human biology originated in one genetic source, led to the suspicion that there was an "integrity and competence" that underlay the Universe: a mysterious greatness that operated in competent

---

[6] Koestler, 686.
[7] Fuller, 298, 300, 303.

patterns in all of nature.[8] In addition, the humanistic belief that the source of inspiration and creativity was in the human brain, was discredited. Experiments with mind-enhancing drugs reveal that creativity does not increase if the powers of the mind are augmented.[9]

All of our scientific advances point to a single source of beauty, goodness and eternal life in the cosmos. This supernal source is a center of light, wave-frequencies, and quanta events; it provides the form (personality) of every soul, and it sends the life-force to inhabit each form.[10] Creativity and inspiration are passed onto the soul when an individual is sufficiently refined in spirituality to receive vibrations from the God-source, the love-source. Because every form contains within it "the patterns of things to come,"[11] creative geniuses like L. Frank Baum, H. G. Wells and Dr. Seuss are often able to see into the future when they create works of genius. Genius is, in fact, the truest expression of the part of us that is connected to the Higher Power.

This concept of creativity as Divine inspiration is not new. Aristotle taught that the soul "was the form of the organism" and that thoughts and ideas had form. Michelangelo told admirers that he was made by God to create: "It is well with me only with a chisel in my hand." That is, his happiness came from creative usefulness.[12] Beethoven kept a motto framed on his desk which read,

I am all that is, was, and will be.
No mortal has lifted my veil.

---

[8] Fuller, 287-289.
[9] Rothenberg, 173.
[10] Still, Judith Anne, "The WWs and World Visions."
[11] Still, Judith Anne, "The WWs and World Visions."
[12] Kees, Bishop Amy, "On Happiness," [Boulder, Colorado: Church of Tzaddi, July 1974] 4.

He is only by himself, and to him alone do all things owe their existence.

Yehudi Menuhin (1916-1999), noted violinist and conductor, told an interviewer that the virtuoso is elected by God to make beautiful music:

> ...There is nothing else he can do. He is compelled to his destiny.[13]

Probably the most articulate artist on the subject of Divine inspiration was William Grant Still. Still offered a lengthy explanation of the interworkings of spirituality and genius in a 1946 interview. He said that genius was characterized by "compassion for his fellow beings," and by the willingness to let "one's musical material...impose its own form."[14]

He continued,

> ...Thoughts are realities. Inspirations or ideas belong to the cosmos; they are universal in their availability to all who can reach out and take them. Some composers can reach higher than others, and for that reason too much credit should not be taken by the individual. Thoughts are realities. God is a reality. As we evolve, God evolves. Life is but a system of governments, each working toward perfection. The process of getting ideas and themes is spiritual, after which the human mind must take over with its inventive and technical ability to put the musical idea on paper, and in the proper form.[15]

Still added that he was successful with his composing because he asked (in prayer) his super-conscious mind to tune into the

---

[13] Brant, 11, 20.

[14] Cook, J. Douglas, "Visits to the Homes of Famous Composers" Series Interview #3: A Personal Interview with William Grant Still, *Opera, Concert and Symphony* 11 [November 1946] 9, 29.

[15] Cook, 9.

"level of inspiration" that was appropriate to the music he was writing.[16]

It is rare to find a composer, a poet, an author, or a dramatist who is so forthcoming about the processes of creation. Other aspects of the process are touched on by Thomas Troward, Helen Wambach, Ph.D., and Evelyn Bull. Thomas Troward (1847-1916), an early teacher of mental science, says that every human being has an inner life, a past life and a potential that can be unfolded and used by the spiritually inclined consciousness.[17] The soul is the part of the individual that connects with the wholeness of the Creator, and which sends inspiration to the artistic person through the subconscious mind.

It is through the subconscious that the creative artist can tap into past-life experiences, past-life accomplishments, and stores of past sensory experiences.[18] And, it is through this access to all of experience that the individual develops his Divine nature, and the ability to transform the earth for the future by using the "principles of the Universe."[19] The individual is aided by the fact that every event and entity in the cosmos is related to every other event and entity, so that every experience that is remembered will set off multiple trains of thought.[20] Through the increasing complexity of thought, it is possible to expand personal potential for creativity; through creative activities, all people are drawn into a progressive spiral toward God, "creating the circumstances for His progressive being."[21]

---

[16] Cook, 9.

[17] Troward, Thomas. *The Creative Process in the Individual* [New York: Dodd, Mead & Company, 1965].

[18] Wambach, 65.

[19] Bull, Evelyn Benham. *Music Therapy: Its Future* [Pasadena, California: Theosophical Society, 1964]; Fuller 286-287.

[20] Barzun, 349.

[21] Bull, *Music Therapy: Its Future.*

It is clear, then, that any individual can affect the development of the human family. But can any individual be a creative genius? There are people whose personalities vibrate at a lower frequency than those who are mature, spiritually, and they can not appreciate the intricate rhythms and patterns of fine music, fine art and elevated literature.[22] They enjoy music with a basic beat, pop art, and pulp novels. A few are quite depraved in their predilections, so that, if they set out to change the world, they do so negatively, as did Hitler and the Nazis. The theosophist Jean Tappendorf explained the gradations of spirituality thusly:

> There is an upward spiraling ladder of spiritual evolution of the soul; wherever people stand on the ladder determines what music, values, ideas they respond to—each person responds to the music that expresses his vibratory level of evolution, his plane of awareness.[23]

To a certain extent, then, people are limited by the frequency of their vibrations when they are born. Yet, all is not lost for those of small capacity for awareness and productivity. While few can alter history as Gandhi did, even the lowest entity on the spiritual ladder can raise his or her vibration to a large extent, and can learn to exert efforts that radiate outward in the invisible world. In the realm of cause and effect, each of us can push himself or herself toward positive causes, and noble effects.

How can this be done? Many approaches are helpful. The first is to attune oneself to the natural world, by going into the country to listen carefully to the sounds of nature. The

---

[22] Still, Judith Anne, "The WWs and World Visions."

[23] Tappendorf, Jean. *Parents' Bulletin, Theosophical Order of Service* 25, [Spring 1960] 1-18.

rhythms of the breezes, the flowing waters, the rustling leaves will raise consciousness and raise sympathetic vibrations. In a like manner, close scrutiny of the heavens at night, and a study of the constellations and the movements of heavenly bodies, will inspire appropriate wonder at the motivating power of the cosmos.

Once an appreciation for the harmony and order of nature is entertained, then persons with simple tastes can begin to listen, every now and then, to the higher musical forms, like those composed by Bach, Chopin, and the like. Pleasing and uplifting concert music itself will act upon the psyche to raise vibratory levels, in the same way that drum beats in a dance will coordinate movements of the dancers. Sophistication of taste often follows sophistication in listening habits. (Attention to music of modernist composers that has more dissonance than harmony is not recommended.[24]) In the same way, refinement can be achieved by going to exhibitions of fine art, preferably art that is not abstract or violent in conception, or by attending plays of a classical or uplifting character. Reading great books, such as Homer's *Odyssey* or Chaucer's *Canterbury's Tales,* is also urged.

The next step up the ladder will be in attempts to tune into inspiration from spiritual sources "in the realm of feeling."[25] It is best to begin this attunement through a non-conscious agency—that is, sleep. The suppliant at the altar of creativity asks, before going to sleep at night, that he or she may receive spiritual understanding and inspiration from the highest sources available to him or her. Care must be taken to ask for communications only from the sources of Divine Light and

---

24 An anonymous writer once said that abstract art is a product of the untalented sold by the unprincipled to the utterly bewildered.

25 Still, Judith Anne, "The WWs and World Visions."

Love. If the person who asks is sincere and self-effacing, there will be instruction for the subconscious mind that comes during the night. Once the channels of communication are open, the individual may move onto the practice of inviting inspiration when awake through quiet contemplation. (Other suggestions for tuning into the Infinite follow in the next chapter.)

The effectiveness of the sleep-technique can be shown by the number of remarkable people who have sanctioned it. Author Shaemas O'Sheel (1886-1954) declared, "He whom a dream hath possessed knoweth no more of doubting." Milton wrote poems in his sleep, and Mozart composed "under the spell of a strong dream."[26] President Abraham Lincoln dreamed of the outcome of battles before the news of the outcome reached him, and he saw a vision in a dream of his own body lying in state after his assassination. Scientist and inventor George Washington Carver (1864-1943) dreamed of the place where he could find a pocketknife that he earnestly hoped to own; when he went to the place, the pocketknife was there exactly as it had appeared in the dream. Writer Gore Vidal (b. 1925) disclosed that he wrote after he woke up, in order to be "closest to the dream world."[27]

William Grant Still composed all night in his sleep, and he received visions of things to come in his dreams.[28] On January 7, 1938, he wrote, "In a dream, I was shown the route ahead, a steady climb to a very high point near the ocean, and then a rapid descent into death valley." It is interesting that his career after 1938 did climb steadily to a lofty height until 1949,

---

[26] Barzun, 341.
[27] Editorial, Interviews with Creative People, "The Creators," 42.
[28] Still, William Grant. *Personal Diary*, February 14, 1945.

when the panning of his opera, "Troubled Island," caused the end of his successes and, essentially, financial inopportunity.

Even so, Still's access to the fountain of inspiration was not blocked, and he continued to produce memorable works between 1949 and 1972, when illness finally brought an end to his compositional efforts. His courage and firm affirmation of the higher good which he served, was proof of the ascendancy of his genius. He was promised in dreams and in messages from psychic mediums, that his works would one day be in the vanguard in the era of spiritual music, as communities "organize and present cultural affairs" on a local level.[29] His music, and great music in general, would "mold the desirable characteristics of the future... ."[30] Music critics, who had once defamed the reputation of Still, would need to become "responsible to higher ideals," and "aware of what art has uplifting qualities."[31]

And how would critics and artists learn responsibility? By promoting only creative efforts that were universal in scope and that appealed emotionally, not intellectually, to all people across the globe. They could not be acceptable to a few persons only—they had to build bridges between styles, cultures and individuals. When popular bandleader and recording artist Mitch Miller (1911-2006) observed that "music is the universal language," he might well have been speaking of all great artistic compositions, paintings, sculptures and plays: their greatness lies in their appeal to all humans made by the Higher Power. And, happily, the greatness of all works of genius is available to all who seek it, waking or sleeping.[32]

---

29 Still, Judith Anne, "The WWs and World Visions."
30 Still, Judith Anne, "The WWs and World Visions."
31 Still, Judith Anne, "The WWs and World Visions."
32 Miller, Mitch, "Over Easy," PBS-Television [October 23, 1980, 7:00 p.m.].

As one scholarly writer said, "One of life's greatest discoveries is that aptitude [and artistic ability] can be expanded, honed and polished, and that ultimate ability is limited by time alone."[33] In fact, says another writer, creativity "is not just for geniuses." We can be creative and productive at any age, and, as we grow older, we find that creativity promotes immune function and calls up positive emotions. "When the mind is challenged, the brain biologically responds in positive ways, regardless of age." In fact, the more we think and do, the more we contribute to vibrant cell life in the brain."[34]

Not only is the brain enhanced biologically and intellectually by our attempts to learn more, to think more and to do more, but the entire body is rendered healthier by productive thought. A researcher and author on nutrition and health, Raymond Peat, Ph.D., tells us that mental activity can increase muscle mass (because the thinking brain uses half of the energy from the food consumed), and it can turn fat in the body to energy for its purposes. More significantly, the ability of persons to visualize can alter the tissues; in fact, Dr. Peat even discovered that it is possible to enlarge the breasts by visualizing that enlargement.[35] The implications of Dr. Peat's discoveries about the mind are that any person, regardless of I.Q., can visualize what he or she wants to do creatively, asking his or her brain and body to help with increased attunement to eternal knowledge, and the result will be a giant leap toward genius. The medical community now agrees

---

[33] Prescott, Wallace S., "To Hinder or Hearten," *Phi Kappa Phi Journal* LII, #3 [Summer 1972] 64.

[34] Cohen, Gene D., M. D., Ph.D., "$C = Me^2$: The Creativity Equation that Could Change Your Life," 33-34.

[35] Peat, Raymond, Ph.D., *Nutrition for Women*, 4th ed. [Phoenix, Arizona: Cenotech Inc., 1981] 91-92.

that the mind can make the body ill; it should also be acknowledged that the mind can make the body well, productive, and, sometimes super-human.

In other words, any sincere effort on the part of any person, no matter how limited in talent, to think and act creatively will change the body, the mind and the course of life itself. As William Grant Still and musicologist J. Douglas Cook expressed it, "Spiritual creativity" can "lift human thought a notch higher in its quest for the all-embracing Truth about itself."[36] Certainly William Grant Still took his first step to a higher level when he wrote, in the late 1920s in Harlem,

> God blesses me. His blessings are many, and great. He has given me the talent for musical composition. Always, after having sought His aid in prayer, themes, far more beautiful than any I could conceive, come freely to me. With them comes a clear leading as to the best way to develop them. ...Because of God's love for me, His blessings, and what I am convinced is the course in life He will have me pursue, I will devote the talent He has given me to efforts designed with intent to glorify Him.[37]

Thus it was that the composer achieved the power, glory and challenge of his great creative genius.

---

[36] Cook, 8.
[37] Still, William Grant. *Personal Journal*, "Testimony."

VIII

<u>Nurture Loving Emotions</u>
Produce with Intensity of Feeling

In these Negro folksongs one may find profound utterances of fear and grief, of the mystery and terror of Negro life, yet composer Still is able to provide this music with that deep, emotional appeal and rich sentiment to make it inspiringly soothing.

- George W. Westerman[1]

I myself believe you have written some of the most impassioned music we possess.

- Frank Calapinto[2]

In order for artistic creations to be valuable, they must provide for the viewer, listener or reader, an emotionally recognizable experience. Edgar Allen Poe (1809-1849) assured us that, "There are chords in the hearts of the most reckless

---

[1] Westerman, George W., "The Passing View," *Isthmain Negro Youth Congress Bulletin*, [December 1943].

[2] Calapinto, Frank, Librarian, National Orchestral Association, New York, Letter to William Grant Still, December 27, 1943.

which can not be touched without emotion."[3] And Michael Hurd added that artistry is not artistry unless it "galvanizes," — it is not just beautiful, it is a personal experience that challenges the onlooker to see the world with "fresh eyes."[4]

Arieti suggested that all great composers expressed emotion through melody, and it was only through melody that emotion could be communicated. Beethoven's music is an excellent example of emotional creativity, for it is passionate, personal, intense, expressive and feelingly profound. When Beethoven spoke about his "Agnus Dei," he said that it was "coming from the heart," and, "may it return to the heart."[5]

The most obvious difference between Beethoven's works and those of 20th century avant-garde composers is in the area of emotion, or in the lack thereof. As George Frederick McKay stated, modernist composers produce music that is "intellectual," written in an "effete mental climate," without "feeling, warmth, emotion."[6] The problem in the last century that gave rise to intellectual culture was the overemphasis on technology and science as the only valid source of creative power. As anthropologist and science writer Loren Eiseley (1907-1977) explained the situation, mankind's discoveries in the sciences increased without a concomitant advance in spiritual growth, so that humans became ashamed of their imaginations and emotional hungers, believing that intuition and feeling did not deal with the same mysteries and truths found in empirical understanding. Thinking people began to mistrust the arts and music, assuming that they had little to do with objective reality.[7]

---

[3] Poe, Edgar Allen, "The Masque of the Red Death," 1842.
[4] Francis, 7.
[5] Arieti, 137.
[6] McKay, Letter to William Grant Still, August 24, 1949.
[7] Eiseley, 388-392.

The rejection of the world of symbols and intuition infected, not just scientific thought, but also the arts themselves. T. S. Eliot (1888-1965) told poets that, if they expressed significant emotions in their works, these emotions would be distilled from their objective observances of other human beings; the writer's own personality and feelings were not properly a part of creativity.[8] In music, composers denounced subjectivity, and began to put compositions together via "mathematical formulae," "specially devised scales," and unstructured combinations of sounds.[9]

What the cerebral artists of the modernist era did not understand, was that future scientific research would eventually uncover a link between the arts and objective existence. Artistic works can change the mental landscape of individuals, rendering them sensitive to others, and to beauty.[10] Literary, musical and graphic symbols can shape personalities and supply power and potential to maturing minds. The influence of certain works of literature, art and music on political and social change (such as Harriet Beecher Stowe's *Uncle Tom's Cabin*, and Chopin's "Polonaise") is incalculable. All artistic expressions that contain emotional ingredients will affect emotional and mental health for good or ill. Significantly, research in psychology has shown that 20% of happiness and success in life comes from one's IQ, but 80% comes through emotional intelligence—the ability to manage one's emotions.[11] Other studies have revealed that reading skills improved if students were permitted to read literature to which they responded emotionally.[12]

---

[8] Eliot, T. S., "Tradition and the Individual Talent," *The Sacred Wood*, London: Methune, 1920.

[9] Still, William Grant, "The Art of Musical Creation," 81.

[10] Eisely, 394.

[11] Goldman, Daniel. *Emotional Intelligence: Why it Can Matter More than IQ*, [New York: Bantam Book, 1995].

[12] Squire, James R., "About Attitudes Toward Reading," *English Journal* 58, #4 [April 1969] 525.

All indications are, therefore, that the vital quality in works of creative genius is in the ability "to arouse emotional responses."[13] Great works will bring a glad and joyful response, and they will uplift the human spirit with love, hope, admiration, and/or the will to emulate that which is uplifting.[14] Even spiritual sources, accessed in occult meetings, have affirmed the absolute necessity for emotion in the arts. Messages in automatic writing sessions, which William Grant Still attended, said,

> There can be no creative arts without feeling and emotion, for these are the expressions of the God-force, or love-force, in life.
>
> *and*
>
> Music and the arts communicate through feeling, and glorify creation by invoking the sense of beauty, peace and hope.[15]

It is for its feeling quality that the music of William Grant Still is so valuable, for, when future studies of the brain quantify the necessity for great art to the preservation of civilization, Still's music will be in the vanguard of those who are fit to fill the need. And then many will say, as George Frederick McKay once confessed,

> I was moved to tears (no less)...by your truly beautiful music.[16]

---

[13] Lloyd-Jones, 262.
[14] Reed, Alfred, "How a Composer Works," 49.
[15] Still, Judith Anne, "The WWs and World Visions."
[16] McKay, George Frederick. Letter to William Grant Still, January 24, 1964.

Nurture Loving Emotions
Hold Fast to Love and Caring

Greatness itself can be measured only in terms of service to humanity.

- William Grant Still[1]

O, God, increase in my heart love for my fellow man.

- William Grant Still[2]

The love that an exceptional person holds for others is greater and more various than the love we speak of for a mate or a sexual partner. It is a force of creative energy, the highest vibration of human emotion. With the power of this love-force comes creative inspiration, the vicissitudes of nature, the life-giving warmth of the sun, the magnetism that attracts entities to one another, the impulse toward fecundity, evolution and growth. It is, in sum, the God-force, for God is love. It is the

---

[1] Still, William Grant, "American Music and the Well-Timed Sneer," 26.
[2] Still, William Grant. *Personal Journal*, "Prayers," #97 and #98.

105

Creator who bestows the gift of creative inspiration upon those who have the spiritual qualities to tap into it.

The all-powerful love-force, which is the essence of God and Creation, has been described in many ways and in differing contexts. Music educator Karl Gehrkens (1882-1975) once sent a letter to all of his friends at Christmastime, 1953, which listed the qualities that pertained to friendship. These qualities could also apply to great people and to the masterworks of genius created by great artists. A friend, said Gehrkens, makes others happy but does not censure them for their imperfections. Such a friend arouses "a warm glow deep down in one's heart," and "the most beautiful light and the most satisfying warmth of any human experience."[3]

Media executive and adviser Roger Ailes made a similar assessment of the qualities of successful leaders in society. He said that the most successful leader is also a very likable person, and one who does not intrude in other people's business unless it is to lend a helping hand to those in need.[4]

Suzanne Bloch, in praising the attributes of her father, classical composer Ernest Bloch (1880-1959), did in fact delineate the attributes of creative genius. She said that her father loved the peace of nature, books, people, family, and that, in all his dealings, he was understanding, tolerant, sympathetic and generous.[5]

---

[3] Gehrkens, Karl, "What is a Friend?" Letter to Personal Friends [Christmas 1953]; Karl Gehrkens gave 35 years of service to public school music education at the Oberlin Conservatory of Music. He also set national standards for training music teachers and was a staunch supporter of music education at the national level through his leadership of several educator associations. Likewise, he authored books, teachers' manuals and was a contributor to music periodicals.

[4] Ailes, 134.

[5] Bloch, Suzanne, "Life With a Musical Father," *Etude* LX, #10 [October 1942] 655, 715.

When aviator Anne Morrow Lindbergh (1906-2001) wrote about the "pure relationship," she was, in fact, speaking of the love-force that is evidenced in the works of the masters. She said that the "pure love" of one person for another is a gift from the Creator, freely given, and it is not bound by present, past, life or time. It is like "the artist's vision before he has to discipline it into form... ."[6] This pure love changes, grows, takes on new forms, and evolves. It "has a pattern like a dance," and a rhythm that nourishes those in love; couples care for one another "in time with the music" of their love.[7] Also, those in love are "in tune with a larger rhythm...between the particular and the universal... ."[8]

Anne Morrow's love for her mate was a rhythmic part of the love of God for man, of the love of God for nature, of the love of humans for coworkers and friends, and of the creative love which infuses the works of artistic geniuses. It is also worthwhile to say that this is the same love-force that underlies the relationship of humans with children, with the natural world and with animals. The love of pets is very much an aspect of greatness, for, according to writer Alice Scott, "Our world's greatest men—statesmen, philosophers, writers, scientists, presidents and kings—were never without the companionship of a dog.[9] Frederick the Great of Prussia had a Great Dane called, "Gengesk," Belgian dramatist-essayist-poet Maurice Maeterlinck adored dogs, especially his pet French bulldog. Abraham Lincoln loved dogs, and even saved the lives of two dogs during his career. William Grant Still had several beloved dogs. The list goes on and on.

---

[6] Lindbergh, Anne Morrow. *Gift from the Sea* [New York: Random House, 1955] 64-65.

[7] Lindbergh, 104.

[8] Lindbergh, 106.

[9] Scott, Alice, "Great Men of History Cherished These Pets," *The Examiner* [Los Angeles, California, November 16, 1957].

Clearly, the ability to love all people and all things, is the most important ingredient of great creative works and great figures in history. But if intelligent individuals wish to develop greatness, though they have not love, can they do it? They can, indeed. Great humans can not only create great works, but also, great works can inspire greatness in those who have it not.

Dr. Grant D. Venerable, educator, chemist and Afro-centric philosopher, tells us that humans are chemical organisms, and that the human physiology changes if attitudes, behaviors and beliefs of humans are altered.[10] Scientists have found that people with multiple personalities will experience major changes in body chemistry when they shift from one personality to another. One personality will require eyeglasses and medication for allergies, while another will not.

Not only will attitudes and behaviors cause changes in brain chemistry, but also emotional stress puts pressure on brain function, because the brain must work to neutralize the effects of tension on the body. The health of the body deteriorates under stress, since stress lowers the immunity to disease. The maladies that are the result of this deterioration have pervasive effects and ramifications: for instance, bladder cancer alters the make-up of a sufferer's urine, so much so that specially-trained dogs can detect its presence by sniffing the relevant eliminations.[11] Unfortunately stress is rampant in today's global population, owing to our habit of processing and refining foods so that vital nutrients are removed from

---

[10] Venerable, Grant D., Dr., "Addict...Artist...Silicon Angel: Charting the Re-Humanization of 'Homo Tectonicus'," Address at California State University – Dominguez Hills [November 18, 1985] 2-9.

[11] Paine, Irene, "Spot the Doc?," *The Spiritual Healer* #602 [August-September 2006].

sugar, flour, cereal, meat, fruit and vegetables. Ergo, the brains of 21st century humans are critically challenged in the attempt to provide compensation for the pervasive malnutrition on all socio-economic levels.

In the end, modern brains are unable to prevent disease and illness — (heart disease, diabetes, lupus, fibromyalgia) — inasmuch as the brain must have sensory stimulation to cope with stress. Sensory complexity is mental nutrition, and it is supplied by education and recreation in the liberal arts. Having removed the fine arts from educational curriculums in the schools, we are discovering that math and science courses do not feed the brain sufficiently to balance body chemistry.[12] The structure and function of the brain adapts "to its sensory experiences." In a "sensory-enriched" environment, abilities to learn and remember are increased, the brain expands in complexity and capability, and mental and physical health follow right along:

> In the human being, the brain does not operate at full power unless it is challenged with tasks of sufficient complexity so that both cerebral hemispheres are fully activated... . Science and mathematics, taught outside the arts/humanities context is a deadly-dull, sensory-deprived exercise in producing brain-damaged people. [A return to the basics of math and science in school, without the humanist's] vision of a unity of diverse parts [makes students victims of hostage syndrome], deprived of the most effective sensory stimulation for coping with the stress levels of the technological age.[13]

Thus, persons who would be extraordinary in accomplishment can cultivate qualities of love and creativity

---

12 Venerable, "Addict...Artist...Silicon Angel" Address.
13 Venerable, "Addict...Artist...Silicon Angel" Address.

by exposing themselves to fine music, valuable pictorial art, foreign languages, good literature and uplifting dramatic productions. They can learn an instrument, memorize famous poems, attend classical theatricals, visit exhibitions of exceptional art, and spend time in museums and historical sites. As long as this regimen of exposure to the fine arts is coupled with a modest exercise program—not aerobic exercise which causes stress, but walking 20 minutes per day which increases memory—along with a balanced diet, the results will be impressive. Dr. Raymond Peat's researches show that "eating good food can alter your consciousness," and raise it to a higher level.[14] (Three healthy meals a day of organic fruits, vegetables, nuts, grains, eggs, fish, unrefined sugar and flour, antioxidants, vitamins, minerals and fiber are recommended.)

The benefits of a natural diet, exercise and a liberal education are beyond measure. The result will be a society of caring, purposeful and courageous primates who have balanced their God-like powers with sensory, emotional and psychological needs. Those who cater to their psycho/socio/emotional needs in this way will become open to the needs of others, and to the love-force that provides inspiration and creativity. As Victorian era thinker John Ruskin (1819-1900) expressed it, "When love and skill work together, expect a masterpiece."

The validity of the liberal arts as a life-sustaining element in the search for heroism can be shown by studies of longevity among singular individuals. Dr. James F. Rogers, in 1929, studied the careers of several hundred famous people who lived between 1700 and 1900, and he determined that, "The great man...is of superior physique and vigor." He noted that

---

[14] Peat, 103.

Bach, Handel and Richard Strauss were actually physical giants, and that all musicians "lived to a comparatively ripe old age, and that their average length of life was greater than that of the rest of the population.[15]

Later, Dr. Gene D. Cohen also investigated the health of important historical figures, and he found that they did not just live longer than ordinary citizens, they also produced great works well after the accepted age for retirement. His report included the following facts:[16]

Galileo was 74 when he published his *Dialogue Concerning Two New Sciences.*

Michelangelo acted as architect for St. Peter's Basilica between the ages of 72 and 88.

Antonio Stradivari was in his 90's when he made two very famous violins.

Giuseppe Verdi composed two great operas at ages 74 and 80.

Noah Webster brought out his *American Dictionary of the English Language* when he was 70.

Winston Churchill was 70 when he finished prosecuting the war against Germany.

Eleanor Roosevelt was instrumental in securing the United Nation's Universal Declaration of Human Rights between the ages of 61 and 68.

Mahatma Gandhi was 77 when he finished his work toward the independence of India.

---

[15] Schweisheimer, Waldemar, M. D., "Do Musicians Live Longer Than Others?," *The Etude* LXII, #1 [January 1949] 24.

[16] Cohen, Gene D., M. D., Ph.D., "C = Me^2: The Creativity Equation that Could Change Your Life," 34-37.

<u>Helen Keller</u> published her book called *Teacher* when she was 75.

<u>Dr. Seuss</u> completed *The Cat in the Hat* when he was 53, and was still writing at 82.

What can be deduced from this study is that the great person does more for a longer time than anyone else in society. In many cases, he or she changes the course of history, and reconstitutes societal ideals and goals. The ability to have such a universal affect on civilized life originates in the receptivity to the universal forces of love, light and creativity, and this ability can belong to everyone. Love is the key, and the fine arts can deliver the key to love and achievement to all of those who wish to follow their noble predecessors into the honored halls of future ages. As William Grant Still asserted, artistry requires,

> [To obtain] what I may call inspiration—not the mood of a moment, but the permanent breath of life, emanating from the Life Source itself.... There are no short cuts and detours, and quick, glittering successes are hardly worth the taking.... But...the opportunities to learn...kept me working harder as my problems grew harder. Eventually, the barriers just fell away. ...And if it happened for me, it can happen for others.[17]

---

[17] Still, William Grant, "The Composer Needs Determination and Faith," 8.

<u>CONCLUSION</u>
Accept the Promise for the Future

There is an unsinkable rule of elevation and longevity where valuable masterpieces are concerned: that which enriches life, no matter how buried in the mud of commercial greed and mediocrity, will one day rise to its proper level in the world's estimation. The plays of Shakespeare were replaced on the stage in the 17th century by the frivolous spectacles called Jacobean drama, and yet, 100 years after Shakespeare's death, his works rose again into view, like a long-immersed continent, never again to lack the praise of millions. Mozart was never fully embraced in his lifetime, overshadowed as he was by envious Salieri, and William Grant Still died without a single widely-available commercial recording of his music. The Resurrection of the artistry of Still is at hand, even as it came for Shakespeare and Mozart. That which is worthwhile ultimately floats above a flood of waste and debris, and carries us on the brimming tide into the future.

It is also mildly pertinent to point out that, just as heroes rise in the public consciousness in the fullness of time, so also do the misguided and self-interested false Gods of a particular period in history fall into the depths of unremarkability. In 1990, thirty years after the period of Marxist unrest on college campuses, a professor named Pinsker wrote a lament in the *Phi Beta Kappa Reporter* bemoaning the lack of concern, in academic circles today, for Communist ideals and causes. In Pinsker's opinion, the professors who promoted Leftist causes in past decades were "critical thinkers" involved in "passionate engagement" of broad public issues. They were, he insisted, imaginative, independent, fearless, heroic, avant-garde and "brilliant." In their lectures, they discussed Lionel Trilling, John Crow Ransom, Harold Rosenberg, Franz Kafka, James Joyce and T. S. Eliot; in their private lives they made time to campaign for a revolt against the American government, and for alienation from capitalistic society and religion.

Pinsker sounded taps for his intellectual heroes, most of whom were dead, retired, or hospitalized as the century ended, leaving their students, who had once seemed to be so involved in their crusade, to sell out in huge numbers to the American free enterprise system. Suddenly the free thinkers were young urban professionals who wanted upscale homes, jobs with benefits, and a way to save Social Security. Pinsker's keening for the ghosts of long-ago Cold War battles fell on apathetic ears, in spite of his warning "that History itself may well end when they do."[1]

It never occurred to Pinsker that the ultra-liberals, who fought so fervently for Revolution in the mid-20th century, may not have been heroes after all, or that their causes may not have been justified. When history does not end, but

---

[1] Pinsker, Sanford S., "The American Intellectual in Unheroic Times," *The Key Reporter* 55, #3 [Spring 1990] 2-4.

political movements do, it is more often an occasion for celebration rather than sadness.

Indeed, much has ended in the 19th and 20th centuries. Slavery fell in the bloody sacrifices of the Civil War, segregation and apartheid followed, the Berlin Wall has gone, and so has Soviet Communism. Next to go will be Communism in China and Korea, and the stagnant era of avant-garde art, modern music, existential drama and unappealing literature. When the public rediscovers harmony and God-given beauty, restoring it to society and to the schools, then the true and necessary revolution will transform and uplift humanity in a spectacular way. When heroes and true creative geniuses ascend from the fallen past and present, having been born or reborn in the recovery of lost artistic principles, then will greatness come again to the earth. As Barzun predicted,

> Rebuilding is bound to come, because true creative power is a phoenix, [and it will rise again in the newly recognized concept of] making something new and making it out of little or nothing.[2]

The great art, music and literature of by-gone ages will sustain us and inspire new creativity and new potential. The work of Mozart, Bach, Beethoven, Rembrandt, daVinci, Michelangelo, Shakespeare, Robert Frost, and all of the other artistic geniuses, has longevity and universality that speaks to all ages and to all peoples, while it builds lofty spiritual bridges between styles, cultures and individuals. As Théophile Gautier (1811-1872), major poet, novelist, dramatic writer and critic of 19th-century France, once said, "All passes. Robust

---

[2] Barzun, 351.

art alone has eternity."[3] The great art of the past will provide enrichment and instruction for our creators of tomorrow; it alone will set the tone for the high art that is to come.

Our future heroes and great men and women will work hard, cultivate diversified interests, live long and fully. They will not be jealous of others; they will not be controlling, spiteful or cruel. They will work for the good of all without idolizing financial gain; they will be humble, courageous and self-affirming.

The chime has been struck by those who have served, and sacrificed and triumphed in the past. The tone is clear and lovely. The striking of the high note is not an event that begins and ends with the notion of the striking—it lasts long afterward in the sustained and captivating vibration. And so it is with immortal human activity and larger-than-life individuals: the vibration lives in those who follow the lead of yesterday's great ones with continued clarity and comeliness. Greatness will grow and prosper again when we, and our children, learn to recognize it for the qualities of emotional truth and harmonious spirituality that live within it and that continue to resonate for us. We can all learn to develop the attributes of great creative genius, for we have the promise of the cosmic life-force that all of us can move, and all of us are moving, in the upward spiral toward creation. Tomorrow exists in our will to achieve at this moment, and, hopefully, the tomorrow that comes shall, as William Grant Still hoped, "hasten the coming of the ideal society wherein every person will devote part of every day to life-sustaining activities, and the other part to cultural pursuits."[4]

---

[3] Editorial, "What Good is Art," *The Etude* LXIII, 38 [August 1945] 423.

[4] Still, William Grant, "The King is Dead—Long Live the King!" *Stadium Concerts Review* (New York) 28, #2 [June 25, 1945] 41.

If each of us seeks to develop at least a few of the qualities of the great geniuses of history, then the ideal society is very near at hand. We have the ability to accept the promise and to enjoy the fulfillment; we have an obligation to posterity and to ourselves to set forth on the path toward that fulfillment.

Steps Toward Becoming
A GREAT CREATIVE GENIUS

Focus, work hard and study widely:

✦ Commit wholeheartedly to your endeavors.

✦ Learn everything you can about the fields in which you have talent.

✦ Practice every day to develop any talents that you have.

✦ Develop interests in a wide variety of things.

Honor your strengths and weaknesses:

✦ Do not spend time trying to do things you are really not good at doing.

✦ DO spend time practicing skills that you have a knack for.

Cultivate good habits of behavior and mind:

✦ Strive to be humble, good-humored, lovable, altruistic and courageous.

✦ Do not settle for convention—think outside the social norm or expectation.

✦ Use common sense—your pursuits must be rational, practical and constructive.

✦ Overcome any pain caused by criticism, envy and opposition. Ignore people who try to demean you, or spoil your efforts.

Exercise your mind:

✦ Do mental exercises, such as word searches and cross-word puzzles.

✦ Learn music, dance, art, drama, debate, languages and writing in order to develop your intuitive skills.

✦ Research practical problems in your home and community and try to develop solutions to them.

✦ Ponder global problems and come up with possible solutions.

Steps Toward Becoming
A GREAT CREATIVE GENIUS cont.

Nurture the health of your brain and body:
+ Undertake 20 minutes of moderate exercise every day.
+ Maintain a positive perspective to enhance your physical health.
+ Eat organic, natural foods; supplement your diet with organic vitamins, minerals, and other nutrients. When ill, consult a licensed homeopathic practitioner.
+ Treat your senses to the masterworks of music, art and literature; work to put music and the arts back into your schools and communities.

Tap into hidden sources of knowledge which exist in the cosmos:
+ Involve yourself in the world around you and actively nurture the environment; join in humanitarian projects and become helpful to plants, animals and nature in general.
+ Ask for spiritual help before undertaking any productive project, then give credit to the Divine Source when inspiration, endurance and accomplishment are realized.

ABOUT THE AUTHOR

JUDITH ANNE STILL
BIOGRAPHICAL AND CAREER NOTES

After becoming a member of Phi Beta Kappa and graduating with high honors from the University of Southern California, Judith Anne Still received a Master of Arts degree as well as secondary and adult teaching credentials from California State University at Fullerton. She then pursued varied careers as an instructor of college English, correspondent for a noted actress of the stage and screen, founder of the Larry Headlee Scholarship Fund (named for her deceased geologist husband who pioneered in mini-submarine operations), and freelance writer. Her many published works have received several awards, including a Washington Educational Press Award, an American Legion Award, and a Freedoms Foundation Award. One of her early articles was read into the Congressional Record. She has authored and/or edited seven non-fiction books, now published, seven unpublished volumes, and numerous published articles and poems. A few of her highly-praised works are *William Grant Still: A Voice High-Sounding* (2003) and "Let Grieving Go" (1975).

As the Director of William Grant Still Music, Judith Anne Still has lectured widely in the United States, and has made presentations in over 200 educational institutions, as well as professional and community organizations. Some of these groups have included the New England Conservatory of Music, the Eastman School of Music, The Governor and Arts Directors of Mississippi, West Point Military Academy, and the Cincinnati Symphony Orchestra. Likewise, she has made several television appearances, including the nationally-televised PBS documentary, "William Grant Still: Trailblazer from the South," and, she has given numerous interviews in radio broadcasts across the United States.

Ms. Still has also maintained active participation in various community projects in the cities in which she has resided. She is the mother of four now-grown children, the grandmother of three, and the long-suffering servant of an ever-growing canine pack.

ABOUT THE COVER ARTIST

DR. GRANT D. VENERABLE II
CAREER NOTES

Dr. Grant D. Venerable II is an authority on the structure and behavior of natural and human-made systems and the early origins of modern systems and organization management concepts. He received a B.S. degree in chemistry from the University of California at Los Angeles, and his M.S. and Ph.D. degrees in physical chemistry/chemical physics from the University of Chicago.

Dr. Venerable carried out post-doctoral research in radiation biology with Lawrence S. Myers, Jr. at the UCLA Laboratory of Nuclear Medicine. He subsequently began his career in higher education on the chemistry, education, and interdisciplinary science and humanities faculties of California Polytechnic State University where he was recognized with a distinguished teaching award. He later fulfilled a successful Sloan Lectureship in chemistry at Oakes College of the University of California, Santa Cruz. As a former Argonne National Laboratory radio-chemist, Dr. Venerable is cited in *Who's Who in America*, and, he is published in such diverse areas as Chemistry, Organization Systems Management, the role of the Arts and Humanities in high-technology societies, African-American Studies, and the Unity of Knowledge.

A National Endowment for the Humanities Faculty Summer Fellowship at Michigan State University was the catalyst for a second career in the Silicon Valley industry. While a systems strategist with Motorola and other high-tech firms, Dr. Venerable became a national spokesman for the arts and humanities in a computer age society. He has spoken extensively at conferences and university campuses in the United States and abroad. He has authored six books, notably *The Paradox of The Silicon Savior*, which provides important insights into our post-modern, silicon chip-based society and its reigning "gods and saviors," as well as *Managing in a Five Dimension Economy: Ven Matrix Architectures for New Organizations*, a systems approach to building and optimizing organizational structure and management.

Dr. Venerable's other administrative posts have included Associate Provost and Professor of Chemistry at Chicago State University; Provost and Vice President for Academic Affairs at Morris Brown College; Chair of the Council of Chief Academic Officers for the six Atlanta University Center Schools; and currently Vice President for Academic Affairs at Lincoln University of Pennsylvania.

Dr. Venerable is a member of the American Association for the Advancement of Science, American Chemical Society, World Future Society, and Alpha Chi Sigma Chemical Fraternity. He has served on the boards of the California Alliance for Arts Education, the Episcopal Church Council at The University of Chicago, and CityQuest of Chicago.

In addition, Dr. Venerable is an accomplished musician and painter, enjoying an international reputation for his oil-on-canvas renderings of molecular structure commissioned by scientists, corporations, and universities throughout the United States, Canada, England, France, and Russia.

COVER DESIGN

Artist's Commentary on
MOLECULAR EXPRESSIONIST ART

I discovered a talent in art even before starting kindergarten, to the extent that my creations won the notice of the District Superintendent. My modest achievements in junior high school earned me a PTA art scholarship to the Los Angeles County Art Institute, where I was inspired by its internationally-renowned master painter, Joseph Mugnaini, to develop my oil on canvas technique. My background in mathematics and science was gained at Manual Arts High School, where I also entered student body politics and served as class president when Judith Anne Still was also a member of our class. (Ms. Still and I were born on the same day, August 31, 1942, and we have been close friends since childhood.)

From high school, I entered the University of California at Los Angeles as a chemistry student. While there, the blackboard drawings of professors Mostafa El-Sayed and the late Kenneth Trueblood moved me to find another "technology" — that of chemical structure and reactions, to portray in oil-on-canvas renderings. When my paintings were shown in the William G. Young Hall of Chemistry, several of my UCLA professors were impressed by them, and commissioned paintings from me of their principal research projects.

My emerging practice of painting the technology of "pure chemistry and physics" continued through my postgraduate studies in the Chemistry Department of the University of Chicago. My notoriety in the world chemistry community increased as I completed numerous works, commissioned by chemistry professors (including two who later won the Nobel Prize), universities, and industrial corporations from the USA to Canada, United Kingdom, France, Germany, and Russia. My first Russian commission, presented to Gregorii Razuvaev at the International Conference on Organometallic Chemistry in

Venice, Italy (1975), proved to be a highlight of the "cold war" between the United States and the former Soviet Union. This presentation of a canvas by an American citizen (of African descent, no less), and, of the world's dominant capitalist power to the head of the scientific academy of the world's dominant Communist power, occasioned the largest gathering of Soviet scientists seen outside the Soviet Union in many years. The irony was not lost on that major assemblage of amazed Europeans.

Over two decades, I have rendered some 300 oil paintings, including dozens of commissioned works. As my understanding of the structure of knowledge and the process of its discovery deepened, I came to a profounder understanding of the meaning of my art: That it is both a process of knowledge mastery and knowledge discovery through a complex act of scientific interpretation, creative imagination, and visual "representation."

If Descartes could say, "I think, therefore I am," my art has taught me, "I create, therefore I am." And if I express in the world what I create, I am connected to the world. I, therefore, belong to that world.

My art—painting and musical performance—is my entry to creativity in all that I do, in science, in educational leadership, and in life.

Dr. Grant Delbert Venerable II
January 14, 2007

Dr. Venerable's work is available for purchase.

Contact William Grant Still Music
at wgsmusic@bigplanet.com for more information.

BIBLIOGRAPHY

Ailes, Roger with Jon Kraushar, "The Importance of Being Likable," *Reader's Digest* 67 [May 1988], 133-135.

Anderson, Harold H., *Creativity and its Cultivation* [New York: Harper & Row, 1959].

Anonymous, "Disagree on Greatest Composer," Los Angeles *Herald-Examiner*, April 20(?), 1940.

Arieti, Silvano. *Creativity: The Magic Synthesis* [New York: Basic Books, Inc., 1976].

Aristotle, *Poetics*, 350 B.C.

Arvey, Verna, "Death of the Etude," *Australian Musical News and Musical Digest* 49, #2 [August 1958].

Arvey, Verna. Lecture to the Swedish Academy, Los Angeles, California [November 15, 1948].

Arvey, Verna. *Studies of Contemporary American Composers: William Grant Still* [New York: J. Fischer & Bro., 1939].

Arvey, Verna, "When Great Musicians Were Boys," *Music World* 2, #4 [September 1931] 12-13.

Bartlett, John. Familiar Quotations [Boston: Little, Brown & Co., 1968].

Barzun, Jacques, "The Paradoxes of Creativity," *American Scholar* [Summer 1989] 337-351.

Bell, Barbara Currier, "Lesson About Learning," *National Forum* LXVIII, #2 [Spring 1988] 33-34.

Bett, W. R., *The Infirmities of Genius* [New York: Philosophical Library, 1952].

Bible, The, Old and New Testaments.

Bloch, Suzanne, "Life with a Musical Father," *The Etude* LX, #10 [October 1942] 655, 715.

Brant, Leroy V., "Genius Begins with Maturity," *The Etude* 71, #11 [November 1953] 11, 20.

Bronowksi, Jacob, "This I Believe," *The Spiritual Healer* [February 2006] 8-9.

Brown, R. Donald. *William Grant Still: An Oral History* [California State University, Fullerton, California, 1967].

Buffington, Perry W., Ph.D., "A Matter of Heroics," *Sky Magazine* [April 1989] 75-79.

Bull, Evelyn Benham. *Music Therapy: Its Future* [Pasadena, California: Theosophical Society, 1964].

Calapinto, Frank, Librarian, National Orchestral Association, New York, Letter to William Grant Still, December 27, 1943.

Carlyle, Thomas, *Westminster Review* #12 [London, 1838].

Chase, Loriene, Dr. "Casebook of Dr. Chase," *Westways* 77 [January 1985] 62-63.

Ciardi, John, *Saturday Review*, December 15, 1956.

Clifton, Donald O. and Paula Nelson, *Soar With Your Strength* [New York: Dell Publishing Company, 1992].

Cohen, Gene D., M. D., Ph.D., "C = Me^2: The Creativity Equation that Could Change Your Life," *Modern Maturity* 43W, #2 [March-April 2000] 32-37.

Cohen, Gene D., M. D., Ph.D., "Contemplating Creativity," *AARP Bulletin* 38, #4 [April 1997] 2, 5.

Bibliography

Cohen, Ted, Ph.D., "Some Philosophical Thoughts About Jokes," *The Key Reporter* 66, #4 [Summer 2001] 4-6.

Cohen, Ted, Ph.D., "A Non-Phi Bete's Comment on Higher Education in America," *The Key Reporter* 66, #4 [Summer 2001] 7.

Colgrass, Michael, "Speaking of Music: The Real Mystery of Salieri," *Music Magazine* 8 [January-February 1985] 38.

Cook, J. Douglas, "Visits to the Homes of Famous Composers" Series, Interview #3: A Personal Interview with William Grant Still, *Opera, Concert and Symphony* 11 [November 1946] 8-9, 26, 29.

Cooke, James Francis, Dr., "The Fabulous Doctor Franklin," Speech to the Kiwanis Club of Philadelphia [January 17, 1956].

Crashaw, Richard, "Saint Mary Magdalene, or The Weeper," 1646.

Denby, Robert V., "ERIC Abstracts and ERIC Indexes: Shortcuts to Creative Writing Documents," *English Journal* 58, #1 [January 1969] 139-144.

DiPirani, Eugenio, "Grasping the Soul of the Composer," *The Etude* LI, #4 [April 1933] 240, 275.

Dirkes, M. Ann, "Only the Gifted Can Do It," *Educational Horizons* 59, #3 [Spring 1981] 138-142.

Donne, John, "Valediction, Forbidding Mourning," 1611.

Donne, John, "Meditation XVII," 1624.

Doris, John L. and Stephen J. Ceci, "Varieties of Mind," *National Forum* LXVIII, #2 [Spring 1988] 18-22.

Douglass, Frederick. *Life and Times of Frederick Douglass* [Hartford, Connecticut: Park Publishing Company, 1881].

Editorial, Interviews with Creative People, "The Creators," *Modern Maturity* 43W, #2 [March-April 2000] 39-44.

Editorial, "What Good is Art," *The Etude* LXIII, 38 [August 1945] 423-424.

Einstein, Albert. *The World As I See It* [New York: Carol Publishing Group, 1991].

Eiseley, Loren, "The Illusion of the Two Cultures," Speech for the Richard Prentice Ettinger Program for Creative Writing [New York: Rockefeller Institute, October 29, 1963] 387-399.

Eisner, Elliott W., "Celebration of Thinking," *National Forum* LXVIII, #2 [Spring 1988] 30-33.

Eliot, T. S. "Tradition and the Individual Talent," *The Sacred Wood* [London: Methune, 1920].

Fetta, Frank, Conductor of the Marina Del Rey/Westchester Symphony Orchestra, California, Comments to the audience at a performance of Still's "Poem for Orchestra," July 2003.

Finneran, John P., "A Tale of Two Dictionaries," *The Freeman* 43 [January 1993] 483-485.

Fleming, Thomas J., *The Man Who Dared Lightening: A New Look at Benjamin Franklin* [New York: Morrow Co., 1971].

Francis, Michael, "The Essence of Creativity: The Michael Hurd Interview," *Talk of the Town* [April-May 1996] 7.

Franklin, Benjamin. *The Autobiography of Benjamin Franklin* [New York: Random House, 1944].

Franklin, Benjamin. *The Life of Benjamin Franklin* (written by himself) [Pennsylvania: Franklin Court Publishing Co., 1794].

Franklin, Benjamin. *Poor Richard's Almanac* [Pennsylvania, 1757].

Fuller, R. Buckminster, "Planetary Planning," *American Scholar* 40, #2 [Spring 1971] 285-304.

Gardner, Howard, "Beyond the IQ: Education and Human Development," *National Forum* LXVIII, #2 [Spring 1988] 4-7.

Gehrkens, Karl, "What is a Friend?" Letter to Personal Friends [Christmas 1953].

Bibliography

Gibran, Kahlil. *The Prophet* [New York: Alfred A. Knopf, Inc. 1923].

Goldman, Daniel. *Emotional Intelligence: Why it Can Matter More than IQ* [New York: Bantam Book, 1995].

Goldman, Richard Franko, "An X to the Left of the Writer," *American Scholar* 36, #1 [Winter 1966-67] 104-106.

González, Nancie L., "Anthropology, History, and the Nature of Evidence," *National Forum* LXIII [Winter 1983] 18-19.

Griffin, Kelly, "Brainpower," *AARP Magazine*, 48, #5B [September-October 2005] 76-78.

Hanson, Howard, Dr., Introduction, *William Grant Still and the Fusion of Cultures in American Music*, edited by Judith Anne Still, 2nd edition revised [Flagstaff, Arizona: The Master-Player Library, 1995] i.

Hanson, Howard, Dr., Keynote address: "A Tribute to William Grant Still," Testimonial Dinner for William Grant Still, Friends of Music, University of Southern California, Los Angeles, California, May 24, 1975.

Henry, Nicholas L., "Hardin Craig, Professor," *American Scholar* 40, #2 [Spring 1971] 305-308.

Herrold, William G., Jr. "Brain Research: Brain-Compatible Learning," *Educational Horizons* 68, #1 [Fall 1989] 37-41.

Hood, Robert E. "Talent," *The Freeman* 31, #7 [July 1981] 399-403.

Horowitz, Joseph. *Classical Music in America: A History of Its Rise and Fall* [New York: W. W. Morton, 2005].

Hubbard, Elbert, "Get Out or Get in Line," *Love, Life and Work* [East Aurora, New York: Roycroft, 1906].

Inge, M. Thomas, "Politics and the American Sense of Humor," *The Key Reporter* 71, #2 [Summer 2006] 8-9.

Kees, Bishop Amy, "On Happiness," [Boulder, Colorado: Church of Tzaddi, July 1974] 1-4.

Keller, Helen. *The Story of My Life* [New York: Dell Publishing Co., 1972].

Kidder-Smith, E. E. KCET-PBS Television, Channel 28, Los Angeles, California [August 2, 1978] 9:00 p.m.

Knecht, William, "Creativity," *Songwriter's Monthly* [September 1993] 11.

Koestler, Arthur. *The Art of Creation* [New York: Macmillan Co., 1964].

Kostelanetz, Andre, "Unforgettable Leopold Stokowski," *Reader's Digest* [January 1978] 101, 103-105.

Kressy, Michael, "The Community College Student: A Lesson in Humility," *College English* 32, #7 [April 1971] 772-777.

Krutch, Joseph Wood, "If You Don't Mind My Saying So...," *American Scholar* 36, #1 [Winter 1966-67] 14-17.

Lapan, Stephen S. *The Meaning of Intelligence: Implications for Gifted Education* [Flagstaff, Arizona: Center for Excellence in Education, 1989].

Lerner, Gerda, "The Necessity of History and the Professional Historian," *National Forum* LXII, #3 [Summer 1982] 37-38.

Lindbergh, Anne Morrow. *Gift from the Sea* [New York: Random House, 1955] 64-65.

Lincoln, President Abraham, Letter to John D. Johnston (Stepbrother), December 24, 1848.

Lincoln, President Abraham, Letter to J. H. Hackett, November 2, 1863.

Lincoln, President Abraham, Letter to Secretary Stanton, July 18, 1864.

Lloyd-Jones, Richard, "Theoretical Problems in Studying Creativity and Composition," *College Composition and Communication* XXI, #3

Bibliography

[October 1970] 261-266.

Marty, Martin E., "Simplify Your Life!," *Reader's Digest* 116, #695 [March 1980] 79-81.

Matthews, Miriam, "Phylon Profile, XXIII: William Grant Still--Composer," *Phylon* 22 [Atlanta, Georgia: Atlanta University Press, Second Quarter 1951] 106-112.

Maurice, John, "Essential Fatty Acids Very Important to Fetus," *The Medical Post* [November 30, 1982] 29.

McKay, George Frederick, Letter to William Grant Still, August 24, 1949.

McKay, George Frederick, Letter to William Grant Still, January 24, 1964.

Miller, Arthur I., "On the Limits of the IMAGination," *National Forum* LXIII, #1 [Winter 1983] 26-28.

Miller, Mitch, "Over Easy," PBS-Television [October 23, 1980, 7:00 p.m.].

Milton, John, "Comus," 1634.

Milton, John, "Paradise Lost," 1667.

Moses, Rudolph, "A Modern Odyssey," *Arts Quarterly* [October-December 1937] 22-23.

Nanus, Burt and Warren Bennis. *Leaders: The Strategies of Taking Charge* [New York: Harper & Row, 1985].

Paine, Irene, "Spot the Doc?," *The Spiritual Healer* #602 [August-September 2006].

Parker-Faye, Bradley. Letter to William Grant Still [September 25, 1974].

Parshall, Gerald and Michael Barone, "Lincoln, To Those Who Knew Him," *U. S. News and World Report* [October 5, 1992].

Peat, Raymond, Ph.D., *Nutrition for Women*, 4th ed. [Phoenix, Arizona: Cenotech Inc., 1981].

Peters, Roger J., "Working Smarter: The Business of Practical Intelligence," *National Forum* LXVIII, #2 [Spring 1988] 12-15.

Peters, Ronald J., "Practical Intelligence," *National Forum* LXVIII, #2 [Spring 1988] 12-16.

Peterson, Dennis L., "Help Wanted: Laborers," *The Freeman* 31, #5 [May 1981] 285-287.

Pinsker, Sanford S., "The American Intellectual in Unheroic Times," *The Key Reporter* 55, #3 [Spring 1990] 2-4.

Poe, Edgar Allen, "The Masque of the Red Death," 1842.

Pope John XXIII [Angelo Giuseppe Roncalli]. *Journal of a Soul* [New York: Doubleday, 1980].

Prescott, Wallace S., "To Hinder or Hearten," *Phi Kappa Phi Journal* LII, #3 [Summer 1972] 64.

Reed, Alfred, "How a Composer Works," *The Instrumentalist* 44, #11 [June 1990] 48-49.

Reno, Doris, "I Compose With Pain I Enjoy," *Miami Herald*, Section E19 [October 29, 1961].

Rivette, Marc, "The Tales of E. T. A. Hoffmann" *Opera and Concert* 13, #8 [August 1948] 16-17, 26.

Roberts, Allen and Juliet Bridgman, "America's Musical Presidents," *Music Journal* XXXII, #4 [April 1974] 16-17, 36.

Roosevelt, Theodore, "Citizenship in a Republic," Speech at the Sorbonne, Paris, April 23, 1910.

Rothenberg, Albert, "Inspiration, Insight and the Creative Process in Poetry," *College English* 32, #2 [November 1970] 172-183.

Rothschild, Alonzo. *Lincoln: Master of Men (A Study in Character)*

Bibliography

[Boston: Houghton Mifflin, 1906].

Schweisheimer, Waldemar, M. D., "Cherubini and Napoleon," *The Etude* LX, #8 [August 1942] 522, 558.

Schweisheimer, Waldemar, M. D., "Do Musicians Live Longer Than Others?," *The Etude* LXII, #1 [January 1949] 24, 54.

Scott, Alice, "Great Men of History Cherished These Pets," *The Examiner* [Los Angeles, California, November 16, 1957].

Smith, Edward C., "Joshua Lawrence Chamberlain: From Antietam to Appomattox," *Lincoln Review* 11, #13 [Spring-Summer 1994] 41-46.

Spencer, Jon Michael, ed. *William Grant Still: A Reader* [Durham, North Carolina: Duke University, 1992].

Squire, James R., "About Attitudes Toward Reading," *English Journal* 58, #4 [April 1969] 525.

Sternberg, Robert J., "Beyond IQ Testing," *National Forum* LXVIII, #2 [Spring 1988] 8-11.

Still, Judith Anne, ed. *William Grant Still and the Fusion of Cultures in American Music*, 2nd edition revised [Flagstaff, Arizona: The Master-Player Library, 1995].

Still, Judith Anne, "The WWs and World Visions" [Flagstaff, AZ: The Master-Player Library, publication pending].

Still, Judith Anne and Lisa M. Headlee, eds., *Just Tell the Story: Troubled Island* [Flagstaff, Arizona: The Master-Player Library, 2006].

Still, William Grant, "American Music and the Well-Timed Sneer," *Opera, Concert and Symphony* 13 [May 1948] 10-11, 26-27, 30.

Still, William Grant, "The Art of Musical Creation," *The Mystic Light* (Rosicrucian Fellowship Magazine) [July 1936] 297-299.

Still, William Grant, "The Composer Needs Determination and Faith," *The Etude* 67 [January 1949] 7-8.

Still, William Grant, "A Composer's Creed," *Music of the West* 17 [October 1961] 13-15.

Still, William Grant, "Horizons Unlimited," *William Grant Still and the Fusion of Cultures in American Music*, Robert B. Haas, ed. [Los Angeles: Black Sparrow Press, 1975] 113-123.

Still, William Grant. Inscription in Dr. Theodore Baker's *A Dictionary of Musical Terms* [New York : G. Schirmer, 1906].

Still, William Grant, "The King is Dead—Long Live the King!" *Stadium Concerts Review* (New York) 28, #2 [June 25, 1945] 7, 11, 41.

Still, William Grant, "Modern Composers Have Lost Their Audience: Why?" *Australian Musical News* [July 1956].

Still, William Grant, "My Arkansas Boyhood," *Arkansas Historical Quarterly* 26 [Autumn 1967] 285-292.

Still, William Grant. Personal Journals, Sketchbooks, Diaries and Correspondence, Estate of William Grant Still and Verna Arvey.

Still, William Grant, "The Structure of Music," *William Grant Still: A Reader*, Jon Michael Spencer, ed. [Durham, North Carolina: Duke University Press, 1992] 173-176.

Swanbrow, Diane, "The Anatomy of Leadership," *USC Trojan Family* 18, #2 [October 1985] 19.

Swanbrow, Diane, "Right, Left Brains May Be Less Different Than We Thought," USC Gazette, *The Trojan Family* 20, #3 [January 1988] 23.

Tappendorf, Jean. *Parents' Bulletin, Theosophical Order of Service* 25, [Spring 1960] 1-18.

Taylor, Deems. "Most of Our Great Symphonies Were Written on Empty Stomachs," *Up Beat* I [January 1939] 9, 16, 26.

Teitelbaum, Sheldon, "The Last Frontier," *USC Trojan Family* 22 [November 1989] 22-28.

Bibliography

Tierney, John, "Quest for Order," *Science 82*, 3, #7 [September 1982] 69-74.

Troward, Thomas. *The Creative Process in the Individual* [New York: Dodd, Mead & Company, 1965].

Turner, Robert, "Bach," *Pavilion*, Los Angeles Music Center [Southern California Symphony Association, Los Angeles, California, 1964] 7-8.

Van Vechten, Carl. Letter to Verna Arvey, September 13, 1943.

Venerable, Dr. Grant D., "Addict...Artist...Silicon Angel: Charting the Re-Humanization of 'Homo Tectonicus'," Address at California State University – Dominguez Hills [November 18, 1985].

Wambach, Helen, Ph.D. *Life Before Life* [New York: Bantam Books, 1979].

Watson, Sir William, "Ver Tenebrosum: Sonnets of March and April 1885," *National Review*, V [June 1885] 484-489.

Webster's Dictionary.

Wells, H. G. *Mind at the End of its Tether* [London: William Heinemann Ltd., 1945].

Westerman, George W., "The Passing Review," *Isthmain Negro Youth Congress Bulletin* [December 1943].

Whitman, Ardis, "That Vital Spark—Hope," *Reader's Digest* 105, #631 [November 1974] 118-120.

INDEX

102, 104
- quote by, 25, 104
Melville, Herman, 7, 67
- work by, 67
Menander, 5
Mendeleyev, Dmitri, 90
Menuhin, Yehudi, 27-28, 92
- quote by, 92
Michelangelo (di Lodovico
  Buonarroti Simoni), 91, 111, 115
- quote by, 91
Michelson, Albert, 90
Miller, Mitch, 97
Milton, John, 13, 22, 32, 76-77, 82,
  96
- work by, 76-77, 82
Mind at the End of Its Tether
  (book), 4
Mitchell, Margaret, 59
Moses (biblical), 44
Mother Teresa (nun), 7
Mozart, Wolfgang Amadeus, 50,
  65-66, 76, 85, 96, 113, 115
musical composition, 9, 11, 19,
  69-70, 76, 77, 84, 92, 99, 103
Napoleon, *see* Bonaparte,
  Napoleon
National Aeronautics and Space
  Administration (NASA), 60
National Association for the
  Advancement of Colored
  People, 49
Nazi(s), 45, 94
Negro History Week, 29
Negro spirituals, 63
Nelson, Boris Erich, 3
Neo-Classic period, 22
Nero, 31
nervous system, 78-79, *see also*
  brain, the human
Newton, Sir Isaac, 56, 90
New York (state of), 56
New York City Center, 4
Nobel Peace Prize, 21, 60
nutrition/malnutrition (effect
  of), 13, 108-109, 110, *see also*

Peat, Raymond, Ph.D.
Oberlin Conservatory of Music
  (OH), 106
O'Sheel, Shaemas, 96
- quote by, 96
Parker-Faye, Bradley, 85
- quote by, 85
Peat, Raymond, Ph.D., 98, 110
- quote by, 110
Perón, Eva, 44, 47
Peters, Tom, 15
Philadelphia (PA), 39, 40, 68
Philadelphia Library (PA), 39
Phillips, Sheila, Dedication page
Philemon, 5
Pinsker, Sanford S., 114
- quote by, 114
Pitt, William, The Elder, 20
Planck, Max, 90
Poe, Edgar Allan, 57, 69, 101
- quote by, 101-102
Pompeia Paulina, 31
Pope, Alexander, 57
Pope John XXIII, 46
Prinetti of Novara, 50
Prussia, King of, 50
Puccini, Giacomo, 58, 76
Pulitzer Prize, 29
Pythagoreans, 80
racism, 34-35
Radcliffe College (MA), 68
Random House (publishing), 52
Ransom, John Crow, 114
Reagan, Ronald (President), 53
- quote by, 53
reincarnation, 88-89
Rembrandt Harmenszoon van
  Rijn, 7, 22, 115
Rogers, James F., Ph.D., 110-111
- quote by, 110-111
Roosevelt, Eleanor, 111
Roosevelt, Theodore (President),
  67
- quote by, 67-68
Rosenberg, Harold, 114
Rossini, Gioachino Antonio, 50